Gentle Reminders for Co-dependents

Daily Affirmations

Mitzi Chandler

Health Communications, Inc.
Deerfield Beach, Florida
www.hci-online.com

Mitzi Chandler
Port Angeles, Washington

Library of Congress Cataloging-in-Publication Data

Chandler, Mitzi.
Gentle reminders : daily affirmations / Mitzi Chandler.
p. cm.
ISBN-13: 978-1-55874-020-4 (trade paper)
ISBN-10: 1-55874-020-1 (trade paper)
1. Meditations. 2. Devotional calendars. I. Title.
BL624.C436 1989
081—dc 19 88–28454
CIP

Publisher: Health Communications, Inc.
3201 S.W. 15th Street
Deerfield Beach, FL 33442-8190

Dana

Nothing is so strong as gentleness,
and nothing is so gentle as real strength.

Ralph W. Sockman

ACKNOWLEDGMENTS

My thanks to my husband, Bob; my sister, Ruth, and my friends, Alice, Armand and Sheilah, for their wise counsel. And to my writer friends who over the years have encouraged me to stop worrying about semicolons and start writing.

INTRODUCTION

NUDGINGS

I believe in nudgings.
Gentle reminders to hold our hands,
guide us toward the unknown,
murmur away our fear.

I believe in nudgings.
Soft words to open our hearts,
lead us from despair,
whisper to us of hope.

I believe in nudgings.
Lullabies to soothe the child within,
awaken us to new beginnings,
sing to us of joy.

I believe in you.

Mitzi Chandler

JANUARY 1

A New Year's resolution is something that goes in one year and out the other.

Resolutions work only for a short while. Our resolve ends about the same time that our set jaws and clenched teeth slacken from fatigue. Miserable from deprivation we neglect what we swore we would do.

Our resolutions fizzle out because they are attempts at changing ourselves from the outside in. Real change happens from the inside out. What we need to do is make New Year's *revelations.*

When these disclosures and discharges cause a genuine change from within, we will truly ring out the old and ring in the new.

I will open my heart and mind to New Year's revelations.

I only ask to be free. The butterflies are free.

Charles Dickens

Mayflies are children of a day. They live only long enough to join in a mating flight held over water and then they die. Without freedom even this simple act of procreation could not take place.

Human beings are infinitely more complex. When our minds or emotions are caged, we aren't able to fully use the natural gifts we brought into this world at birth, nor will our souls learn how to soar.

Recovery is the process of freeing our bodies, minds and souls from the cocoon of the past.

It is no small thing that I want to be free. I will become all I can be in mind and spirit.

JANUARY 3

Beyond a wholesome discipline, be gentle with yourself. You are a child of the universe, no less than the trees or the stars; you have a right to be here.

From Desiderata

If ever there was a message that co-dependents need to take to heart, it is the one above. We are so hard on ourselves.

As children most of us had a favorite stuffed animal, one who we loved above all others. In time its fur wore thin, it lost a button eye, its seams split and it slowly lost its stuffing. But it remained our favorite — all the more because it was imperfect. We loved it to death.

Like a tattered doll, the Child Within needs our gentleness, our concern, our loyalty. It needs to be loved to life.

Today I will treat myself with gentleness.

JANUARY 4

Patience is power. With time and patience the mulberry leaf becomes silk.

Chinese proverb

Silk worms spin a cocoon to contain them while they hang from a twig in a dormant state of development. These strong, elastic filaments of silk are then processed into beautiful fabrics.

In the same sense, those of us from alcoholic homes spun a cocoon to protect the most precious part of ourselves — our feelings — and we went into a dormant state of survival. Now fully grown, we can patiently weave the raw material of our cocoon into a blend of strong, pliable, vibrant emotions that reflect the richness and shimmer of silk.

With time and patience I will become all that I was intended to be.

The shell must break before the bird can fly.

Alfred, Lord Tennyson

By the time we seek professional help or attend our first self-help group, our shells already have hairline cracks. What has been encased in denial is beginning to ooze out, and we don't know what it is or what to do about it.

Therapy and self-help groups provide a favorable environment for development — an incubation period — from which we slowly emerge from our encasements. We struggle from within, tap at the shell that protects but confines us, and little by little we break through to the surface. Now free of the shell, we learn to move. And when the time is right, we spread our fledgling wings and fly.

Today I will soar!

If at first you don't succeed — try reading the instructions.

On attending our first support group meeting some of us think we have it all figured out before we have our second cup of coffee. We half-listen to what is said then volunteer to share — right from the bottom of our head. "This is easy," we declare to ourselves. "I'll go home tonight, wind the clock, put the cat out and do the Steps." What we manage to do in this state of denial is go home, wind the cat, do the clock and put the Steps out.

A few months or years later we return. We listen to the Steps, to the sharing, and we listen to the small voice from within our hearts. And we know that this time we will start at the beginning and do it right.

God, grant me the wisdom to say the Serenity Prayer.

Great tranquility of heart is his who cares for neither praise or blame.

Thomas Kemper

When we are encased in serenity, we are self-contained units. Our Higher Power provides us with everything we need to feel fulfilled and at peace.

This is not to say that we don't want to be held in esteem by others, nor that we are impervious to rejection.

When we have serenity, we have the ability to run such matters through our emotional and spiritual circuits without excess build-up or break-down.

To keep our serenity in good working order requires that we let go of people and situations that are not ours to hold, and to cling to faith in ourselves and our Higher Power.

With the help of my Higher Power I am finding withirr myself everything I need to be whole and serene.

JANUARY 8

We see through others only when we see through ourselves.

Eric Hoffer

There is an expression: "It's as plain as the nose on your face." Well, is the nose on your face that plain? If we look cross-eyed, we see two images of our nose, or depending on which eye we close, we get either a left or right glimpse of the tip of it.

As children from dysfunctional homes, we had to rely on the adults around us to tell us what our nose looked like and what our feelings felt like. And as their view was distorted, we received information that was not accurate. By the time we were old enough to look in the mirror to see for ourselves, we didn't see who or what was really there, we only saw and felt the distortions.

Recovery is a magic looking glass. And when we see ourselves, seeing others is as plain as the nose on our face.

Each day I am learning more about who I really am.

Time is a dressmaker specializing in alterations.

Faith Baldwin

The advice, "A stitch in time saves nine," comes a bit late for co-dependents. Our seams are quite frayed by the time we put ourselves in the shop for repair.

We enter recovery worn thin, faded and musty from neglect. Our emotions are stretched and shapeless from hanging in the closet of denial for so many years. We are in need of alterations from the best hands available, the hands of a Higher Power.

With time our wounds slowly mend. Our emotions are altered, brought up to date and coaxed into shape with the help of these healing hands. And when they have completed their work, we reenter our world almost as good as new.

Today is a time of repair and renewal.

JANUARY 10

The process of maturing is an art to be learned, an effort to be sustained. By the age of 50 you have made yourself what you are, and if it is good, it is better than your youth.

Marya Mannes

Those of us from dysfunctional homes had a few road blocks placed in the way of our emotional maturation. But even at 50 (and then some), it is not too late to get around those obstacles and grow. And it will be good. Most certainly it will be better than our youth.

It is natural to be concerned that perhaps we'll never catch up in maturing. But this isn't so. As children we often functioned as adults, and we did it well. People described us as wiser than our years. And we were. We had to be to survive.

We cannot get back the years lost to us, but we can live the years ahead fully and deeply enough to make the whole journey worthwhile.

Each day I grow in maturity and wisdom.

JANUARY 11

Never try to catch two frogs with one hand.

Chinese proverb

There are co-dependents who come to recovery programs and in two hops and a leap believe that they have it all figured out. They are cured, warts and all.

When we are further along in recovery, we know that healing is a slippery thing, hard to hold on to if we take on too much at once. We learn that recovery is a little hop at a time from one pad to the next. And we know that we sometimes miss and go "plop" face first into the pond.

Grasping one frog at a time is enough work for any hand, even with the help of a Higher Power!

I will take it one frog at a time.

JANUARY 12

You're only young once. After that it takes another excuse.

When we were children and the sky started to fall on our heads, we went undercover. Smart thing to do at the time. But we forgot to come out, forgot *how* to come out.

Some of us crawled out, stood up, looked at the sky and discovered it wasn't falling anymore, although we were still afraid that it might. We told our friends that the sky wasn't falling, and they believed us. But they, too, were still afraid that it might.

We began to talk with each other, join hands, ask a Higher Power to help us not be afraid anymore. We made rivers from tears, fire from anger and let go of our past. In the process, we learned to forgive others and learned to love ourselves.

Today I stop making excuses that interfere with my recovery.

JANUARY 13

I have seen the future and it works.

Lincoln Steffens

When we open the doors of our past, when we begin to heal, it seems as though our feelings go from bad to worse. And they do. Up until now, our pain has been numbed, diverted, misplaced or disguised. To heal is to grieve with the lost child huddled inside the dark of ourselves. It takes time. It takes patience. It takes hope.

When we become discouraged and feel that we can't go on, it is helpful to look at the faces and hear the voices of those who are further along in their healing.

As we travel toward the future, we will shed our pain a little at a time.

When I am hurting, I will look to others who are further along in their healing and know that I am on the same journey to health and happiness.

JANUARY 14

I don't know who my grandfather was. I am much more concerned to know what his grandson will be.

Abraham Lincoln

As children we are handed down what we are handed down. The end. Period. There is nothing we can do about that. But the buck stops here. With us.

Now that we are as tall as we're ever going to be, it's up to us to make the most of who we are and where we're going.

To recover from our losses is to *go through* grief — pitch a tent for a while — then move on. To *work through* anger is to let the molten lava flow to the sea to build, not destroy.

Recovery is hard work. We need the support of others and the loving hands of our Higher Power.

I will be responsible for who I am and where I am going. I will ask for help when the going gets tough.

JANUARY 15

We are not amused.

Queen Victoria

We can go through life with a pinky in the air, scoffing at silliness, frowning at fun. That's okay, there's no crime in it. But there's also no joy in it. No falling-down-with-laughter delight in being alive.

Philosophers say that a great person is one who has not lost the ability to be childlike: playful, creative, spontaneous, curious, open. Once-upon-a-time we had that "greatness." But due to circumstances beyond our control — living in addictive homes — we had to tuck those fantastic qualities away along with fear, anger and hurt.

We can recapture our greatness.

I will seek the company of people who twinkle, so I can learn to be playful.

JANUARY 16

Some people stay longer in an hour than others can in a week.

William Dean Howells

Some people give off vibrations that bite. Ears back, fangs bared, they sink their negativity into our hides and hold on. And like fools, we stand still and let them.

We have choices when being confronted by negative people. We can stay with them until our ears droop, bite back or high-tail it out of there. Or by our example, we can teach them new tricks — like how to be positive. In extreme cases, we have an obligation to put a muzzle on them.

I will not allow negative people to ruin my day.

JANUARY 17

If the first button of a man's coat is wrongly buttoned, all the rest will be crooked.

Giordano Bruno

Some mistakes are easy to correct. They are of no consequence. Other mistakes are merely stepping stones to learning to do something well. But if our attitude is mistaken — wrongly buttoned — then the whole fabric of our life will be out of alignment.

Attitude is the first button to all aspects of well-being. When attitude is buttoned in resentment, we will imagine slights that were not intended, hold grudges and scowl until our faces are crooked. But when attitude is buttoned in growth, then we have the ability to unfasten what is askew and start again.

I will look at my attitude and change it for the better.

Here we have a baby. It is composed of a bald head and a pair of lungs.

Eugene Field

We come into this world with our bald head ready to be filled with knowledge and our lungs ready to breathe in the wonder of life. We are also helpless. We are at the mercy of the giants who look down at us.

If born into a family where nurturing is abundant, our needs are met consistently and tenderly. If nurturing is lacking or sporadic, fear and confusion short our receptors, and we begin to malfunction.

We sputter into adulthood held together with makeshift parts. The first miracle is that we make it in the condition we're in. The second miracle is as adults, we are not helpless any longer. We can begin to mend our brokenness.

Today I will feel brand new.

JANUARY 19

I wasn't over my skates.

Debi Thomas

There are days when everything seems to slide out from under us, nothing goes right in spite of our best efforts. We become discouraged, tired of trying, want to hang our skates up for good.

Winners learn from their mistakes and go on. With a boost from the coach — our Higher Power — we can pick ourselves up, put one foot in front of the other and get back into the arena.

Today I will do my best. I will learn by my mistakes and go on with a positive attitude.

When angry, count to four. When very angry, swear.

Mark Twain

To many of us, anger is a four-letter word and then some. As children, we saw anger misused and overused. We enter adulthood frightened of this emotion, and have learned to cover our own anger with depression, self-pity or numbness. Or we follow the example of our caretakers and go right to rage at the slightest provocation.

Anger is a God-given emotion. Our task is to relearn when and how to express it, and to what degree. We can use it to clarify or muddle, to heal or destroy.

Anger is a five-letter word that spells r-e-l-i-e-f when used appropriately, and t-r-o-u-b-l-e when used inappropriately.

When I feel angry, I will express it directly and honestly in a way that benefits my life and the people in it.

JANUARY 21

The tongue of man is a twisty thing.

Homer, Iliad

Gossip is a cheap fix. It temporarily blots out whatever inadequacy we feel. But nobody can stop with one juicy bit of gossip. We have to have another and another to dull the pain. And as we become drunk on gossip, our tongues thicken, and twist the tidbits to suit our needs.

Those that hang on the grapevine are a withered lot. A Gaggle of Gossips are never *for* anything. They bunch up *against* things and people.

It is human and understandable to want to dull our hurts, fill our emptiness. But gossip is a poor, ineffective way to do this. We have not built ourselves up, only torn someone else down.

Today I will hold my tongue if I feel the need to make myself seem better at someone else's expense.

JANUARY 22

Little boats should keep near shore.

Benjamin Franklin

When bouncing over the troubled waters of healing, it is wise to take precautions. Stay near shore, sound the fog horn, put out the SOS, call in the Coast Guard — your Higher Power.

It's a big ocean to cross and there will be fierce storms along the way. There will be days when the engine quits, and days when the fog is too thick to navigate. These are the times to drop anchor and find a quiet harbor until it is safe to begin the journey again.

As we grow we can begin to venture into the open sea, more sure of the strength of our vessel, more aware of the direction in which we're heading.

I will use caution in my healing and not take on too much at once.

JANUARY 23

Loneliness is not so much a matter of isolation as of insulation.

Rev. Harold W. Ruopp

Many of us became masons out of necessity when we were young. We troweled mortar onto brick in a desperate effort to survive. And though lonely, we survived with our feelings sealed away for safekeeping.

By the time we are adults, we are accustomed to isolation. We don't know any other way to be. We have built our wall so thick, insulated it so well, that no air circulates and our feelings wither and all but die. We have sealed ourselves off, even from ourselves.

Emotions *are* life. Without them, all of them, we come up empty, and go down lonely.

Today I will begin to break through the barriers that make me lonely.

Did you ever think that what Fred Astaire did, Ginger Rogers did it backward and in high heels?

The Grand Waltz of Life is difficult at best. In a healthy home, a child is guided with patience, discipline and love from the first simple steps of the dance to the more complex twirls and dips.

Coming from homes where patience, discipline and love were sporadic or nonexistent, we had no choice but to stumble through the dance, feeling always as though our shoes were on the wrong feet. We entered adulthood tripping backward.

The miracle is that we can teach ourselves to dance. With effort, we can progress from the simple two-step of survival to waltz with grace — in any direction.

I will waltz through this day the best I can, knowing that tomorrow I will know the steps even better.

Why do birds sing in the morning? It is the triumphant shout: "We got through another night!"

Shadows are the creatures of the night, elusive forms we sense more than see. We hear the rattle of old bones and the whisper of voices from the past, feel the cold fingers of an uncertain future. The dark closes in on us.

Yet the night holds wonder and promise. In a distance farther than we can grasp, stars pulse with life. And as if for the sheer joy of it, some sizzle like sparklers as they shoot through the dark. As the moon moves across the sky, it casts a soft glow over the earth and we are comforted by the light.

Fear and peace, weakness and strength, doubt and spiritual hope are the dark and light of our emotional world. Without one feeling, we could not appreciate the other.

I will accept my humanness and be comforted knowing that I am on a spiritual journey.

JANUARY 26

Hatred is self-punishment.

Old proverb

When you remove the letter *B* from *blame* you are left with the word, *lame.* Blame, resentment, revenge and self-pity are crippling feelings. When we hold on to them, we are forced to limp through life, handicapped by our inability to love.

The underlying cause is hate. Its venom poisons everything we feel or don't feel. Coiled, it strikes at anything that comes too close to something that lies even deeper within us.

That something is hurt, a deep childhood hurt we think too painful to feel. Little care was given to this wound and it festered into a hot swollen mass called hate.

We don't have to continue in this self-punishment. We can begin to unwrap the layers that cover this old wound and let it feel the healing touch of love.

I can feel the hurt of abandonment and rejection and now recapture my ability to love.

JANUARY 27

You might as well fall flat on your face as lean over too far backward.

James Thurber

There is such a thing as being too helpful.

Are we trying to buy love when we lean over backwards in our helpfulness? Are we trying to control others? Are we afraid to say no to a request for help for fear of rejection? Or are we being helpful because we sincerely want to?

Groveling for love through helpfulness doesn't feel good inside. It robs us of self-respect. Controlling others with our helpfulness makes them resent us. And we get angry at ourselves when we can't turn down a request for something we don't want to do.

When we are helpful for the sheer joy of it, we get something whole and healing. There can never be too much of that kind of helpfulness.

I will be helpful only in ways that hasten my recovery.

JANUARY 28

I came. I saw. I conquered.

Julius Caesar

When we come to recovery programs, we have placed ourselves in an atmosphere that helps us to see what the problem is. To conquer and overcome our pain is up to us. But we are not alone. We have the support and heartfelt understanding of others who have experienced our dilemma and discomfort. And we have the healthy example of those who have been in recovery longer than we have. And when we are ready, we can reach out for the loving help of a power greater than ourselves.

With the help of others and my Higher Power, I can overcome the pain of my past.

JANUARY 29

Hasten slowly.

Proverb

To be excited about growth, to anticipate what will be, is wonderful. But to be anxious about it, be impatient with its slow steady pace, be consumed about tomorrow, is to lose sight of the miracles that have already occurred in our healing. To grow "one day at a time" is a wiser and easier path to recovery than trying to accomplish it all in one fell swoop. This hastening will lead to burn-out and backsliding.

Winter gives way to spring quietly with a warming of the air, melting of snow, opening of blossoms, the return of robins, the buzzing of bees. And as if all in one moment, the miracle happens and the world is in bloom. Spring has hastened slowly toward its full beauty. This is the way of growth.

I will savor each day with a grateful heart. I will let tomorrow happen tomorrow.

JANUARY 30

Come, my friends, 'tis not too late to seek a newer world.

Alfred, Lord Tennyson

'Tis a miracle that we can go back and fix what was broken. 'Tis a miracle that we can fix it so well that it becomes better than it might have been in the first place.

Many old-timers in 12-Step programs say that they are grateful for everything that happened. It is hard for those who are hurting to understand how anyone can feel grateful about suffering. What these seasoned folks are saying is that their lives have a depth and breadth that they might not have had without the suffering. They are saying that they have connected with a life force greater than themselves and are at peace.

" 'Tis a grand thing to be given a second chance."

Today is not too late to find happiness.

JANUARY 31

Think of the beauty still left around you and be happy.

Anne Frank

Childhood is prime time for development of intelligence and natural abilities, formative years for learning how to get along with others. And during those early years is when we form opinions and attitudes about who we are and what this world is about. Adult Children have lost large portions of their childhood.

Some of that loss is salvageable. Recovery allows us to go back and fix what is fixable and accept what is not. And out of our wreckage, we can create uniquely beautiful human beings.

Today I will not dwell on what I have lost, but be happy with the beauty I am finding in recovery.

Early to bed and early to rise, makes a man healthy, wealthy and wise.

Benjamin Franklin

The human body is always trying to right itself when we wrong it. We serve as parent to all the tiny cells in our body. When they are provided with the proper food, exercise and rest, they function well. But when we neglect or mistreat them, they have no choice but to protect themselves. In time, these overworked protective mechanisms break down and so do our maligned bodies.

As we recover the broken pieces of our emotional selves, we need to provide a healthy place to keep them. Learning about, and practicing the proper care of our bodies goes hand in hand with the healing of our psyche and soul.

My body houses my mind and heart. I will treat it with respect and provide it with what it needs to be healthy.

FEBRUARY 2

People often say that this or that person has not yet found himself. But the self is not something that one finds. It is something that one creates.

Thomas Szasz

Like artists painting portraits, we create ourselves a stroke at a time by our actions and choices. We determine the source of light and the length of shadows in our lives. We can paint our portraits in muddy colors or vibrant hues. We can be daring and bold in our strokes or timid and afraid to venture beyond what is familiar. And when we wait patiently to catch the light, we are given the opportunity to see beneath the surface and behold our spiritual selves. This vision allows us to dip our brushes into our souls and recapture that beauty in our lives.

Each day is an opportunity to grow and become more whole. I want my life to be rich with color and bathed in light.

FEBRUARY 3

The worst loneliness is not to be comfortable with yourself.

Mark Twain

When we reject who we are, we are forced to live with a person we consider unworthy. Or more miserable yet, a person we hate. This terrible discomfort is the crux of the matter for co-dependents. When we reject who we are, we have lost our best friend.

We came into this world with smiles in our hearts, wiggles in our toes and floppy little hands ready to grasp at life and love. In the chaos of our childhood this joy slowly eroded and an unspeakable discomfort and loneliness set in. This was not fair but it happened.

Today we have a choice to remain miserable or to go back and comfort our original selves. It is up to us to become our own best friends and rid ourselves of gnawing loneliness.

I have a right to be comfortable with myself. I have a right to reclaim the precious child that a power higher than myself created.

FEBRUARY 4

Tell me thy company and I'll tell thee what thou art.

Cervantes

A grape has no choice. If it is unfortunate enough to be bunched up beside a rotting one, it too will rot before its time. Nearby grapes will pick up the acrid taste of their neighbor, but those dangling further away will remain sweet and plump.

We have a choice. If we choose to hang around with a bunch of decaying folks, it's going to rub off. We don't help others by rotting with them.

I will choose to be with people who help me grow, not decay.

As soon as you trust yourself, you will know how to live.

Goethe

Healing is a hodgepodge of inner conflicts working their way toward truth. Early in recovery we are baffled and bewildered by this process. "What's happening to me? I'm losing control!" is the lament of the co-dependent who has begun the arduous journey toward health.

Losing control is the point. It is the fulcrum that unravels denial from reality. In the unraveling we learn the how and why of our behavior, our co-dependency, our loneliness. And in the unraveling we slowly begin to trust our feelings.

While we are in the early throes of recovery, it is helpful to heed the words of those who are further along when they say, "Trust the process."

I am learning to talk, feel and trust.

A diamond is a piece of coal that stuck to the job.

Recovery shows. It sparkles from the eyes of those who have been freed from the bedrock of their past. The healing process has served as a gem cutter, tapping, tapping at the uncut stone until pieces fall away and the light that is encased inside bursts through. Unique, exquisite, of great value.

In each of us a dazzling light waits to be freed. It has always been there, we were born with it. It need only be tapped.

With the help of my Higher Power, I will find my light.

FEBRUARY 7

Behold the turtle. He only makes progress when he sticks his neck out.

James Bryant Conant

It is noble to stick our necks out — come what may — and risk the consequences. But if someone is brandishing an ax over our shells, prudence would have us hold the urge to stick our necks out until the danger is less final.

Knowing when to risk and when to protect ourselves is part of recovery, part of learning about discretion and boundaries, part of self-preservation. In our denial we have become rusty at these skills.

In our daily lives and in healing there are times to give it your all, your daring, your best shot. There are times to take a break, pull back and use caution. And there are times to turn around and run for your life. Progress has three gears: forward, neutral and reverse. Recovery is knowing which gear to use when and for how long.

I will learn the difference between taking risks and being foolhardy.

FEBRUARY 8

Be comforted. You would not be seeking Me if you had not found Me.

Ovid

When we were small and had to tuck our feelings away for safekeeping, many of us also folded into deep pockets the elusive thing called spirituality. As we now begin to unfold the cloth of our lives, reaching through the layers of denial, we rediscover the precious items we have stored away. Often the last to be unfolded is spirituality.

This is why doubt about God, or a Higher Power, is prevalent among co-dependents in the early stages of healing. It takes time and pain to sort through the layers of our past. And it is a leap of faith to accept what others further along in recovery tell us about spirituality.

Today I will be comforted, knowing that I am on an inward journey in search of my lost self and my Higher Power.

FEBRUARY 9

I never had frustrations;
The reason is to wit:
If at first I don't succeed,
I quit!

Some people are quitters and others wouldn't quit if their lives depended on it. Somewhere in that vast middle lies the answer to success.

Frustration is part and parcel of being alive. If we expect that obstacles will present themselves, that we may not be able to do whatever it is we are trying to do perfectly, that Murphy's Law will prevail much of the time, then we will not be bullied by frustration. We can use its energy to try and try again, rather than throw our hands in the air and proclaim, "I quit!"

I will not quit a task at the first frustration, nor will I stick to something that is beyond reason to do so.

FEBRUARY 10

And what is a weed? A plant whose virtues have not been discovered.

Ralph Waldo Emerson

Many Adult Children feel like weeds. Unwelcome, unsightly intruders on the landscape, who will be pulled up and left to rot on the compost heap.

This does not have to be our fate. If we allow the hands of the Great Gardener to sprinkle the rain and sun of healing on our hearts, we can begin to grow and discover the wonder and virtue of ourselves.

I will ask my Higher Power to help me blossom and become all that I can.

FEBRUARY 11

A person offering to help a blind person across the street: "May I go across with you?"

When we are exposed to tact, we know that we have just been hit with something kind, but are not always sure what it is. Tact is subtle. It can make nice things nicer, and unpleasant things bearable. A person blessed with tact is a person well-blessed.

To be tactful is to think clearly, to be sensitive and to have the other fellow's welfare in mind as well as your own. As our self-esteem grows, and we are not on constant vigilance, not turned so inward, we automatically become more gracious, more sensitive to what is going on around us. We do not react as quickly, therefore, we are more able to "act" with delicacy and tact.

Today I will try to be tactful in my dealings with people.

FEBRUARY 12

You ain't heard nothing yet, folks.

Al Jolson

When we have been depressed, repressed or just plain miserable most of our lives, we have only an inkling of what it's like to be content and at peace with ourselves. And when those first bursts of well-being hit us, we think we have "arrived." But it is just the beginning.

As the days spill over into months, into years, a slow, steady process takes place. It has highs and lows and resting places. With our assistance and willingness to feel the pain buried inside, it continues forward toward self-discovery and self-love. Each time we deal with unfinished business (and this requires us to hurt), we are given a precious gift.

I will be open to the pain of healing knowing that I am on a journey toward happiness.

FEBRUARY 13

My anger is 41 years old . . .

Adult Child

When young, many of us were not able to express and work through angry feelings. So they simmered, turned thick and dark, became a cauldron of poison. We carry this vat full of anger into adulthood with us.

We are afraid that if we begin to express our outrage at what happened to us as children, we will lose control. And we feel that if we are angry, then we are not good persons. So left to seethe, anger turns to self-pity, self-hate or depression and slowly eats away at the vessel that holds it.

It is not an easy task to lift the lid off anger, but if we accept that working through it is necessary for recovery, we can begin to express it in constructive ways. To acknowledge it is to let it evaporate.

I will accept my anger and begin to use it in ways that benefit my healing process.

FEBRUARY 14

Love is, above all, the gift of oneself.

Jean Anouilh

Most of us have been pierced by Cupid's bow and experienced the magic and madness of falling in love. But, alas, most of us learned that the wonder and intensity of romantic love are not lasting. What happens after the honeymoon is what genuine love is about.

New love is the gift-wrapping shimmering with promise. Lasting love is the gift inside — the slow unfolding of our deepest selves to the other. We must trust, risk and expose our frailty and vulnerability as well as our strengths. When we do this, we give our partner the most precious part of ourselves — our humanity. And in this giving we are blessed.

I am learning to love myself so that I can bring genuine love to my relationships.

FEBRUARY 15

When I do good, I feel good. When I do bad, I feel bad. That's my religion.

Abraham Lincoln

One of the most difficult tasks for just about everyone is to keep things simple. Our brains take over and apply abstract formulas and complexity to life's issues, great and small. In our civilized world we value the answers in the mind more than we value the answers in the heart.

When we begin to listen to our feelings, as well as our logical thoughts, we are on our way to simplifying. And when we simplify, we hit upon clarity. And when we are clear, there is no complexity, only easily understood one-day-at-a-time simplicity.

Today I will keep it simple.

. . . He is all fault who hath no fault at all. For who loves me must have a touch of earth.

Alfred, Lord Tennyson

Some of the most delightful people around are those riddled with "faults." They have an ease about them, they laugh at themselves and their foibles. They know that life is too serious to take themselves seriously. Their shortcomings endear them to others.

And then we have those who strive for perfection in everything they do.

They set up extremely high, inflexible standards and when they fall short of these impossible goals, they berate themselves and try even harder. This behavior is self-defeating and takes the fun out of life.

I will correct the faults that are harmful to myself or others, and accept my benign shortcomings as a lovable part of my uniqueness.

Do you ever get the blues? No, I give them!

Self-pity stifles. It's like holding the brake down while trying to move forward, going nowhere fast. A person stuck in this gear finds solace in making others suffer with them.

Self-pity is an attitude that makes growth impossible. Until we can accept that it isn't what happened to us, but what we do about it, we will wallow in past grievances and create new ones each day.

We deserve better. Why be our own worst enemies? Why stay bogged down when there are better ways to deal with pain and disappointment? It is scary to give up this defense and face what needs to be faced in ourselves, but it is better than singing the "Poor Me Blues."

I will stop dwelling on the misfortunes in my life and see what I can do about them.

FEBRUARY 18

The world goes up
And the world goes down,
And the sunshine follows the rain;
And yesterday's sneer and
Yesterday's frown
Can never come over again.

Charles Kingsley

The best way to ruin a brand new day is to stumble toward the kitchen and pour a cup of yesterday's bitter coffee. With a little more effort, we could make a fresh pot, one more worthy of the new day.

There are past issues to be dealt with. Working through these issues is a different brew than sipping on grudges and gulping down self-pity. Our new day hardly has a chance when we greet it in this manner.

We need to pour out what is old and acrid, start anew and fill our cup with sweet serenity.

This is a new day given to me by my Higher Power. I will let go of bitterness and seek serenity.

FEBRUARY 19

Some people walk in the rain, others just get wet.

Roger Miller

Children have the knack of finding delight in everything around them. Sloshing through puddles, drawing pictures on foggy windows, keeping time with the car windshield wiper are grand events to a child.

Somewhere along the way most of us lose the ability to experience joy in ordinary things. We need more and more stimulation to feel excited and alive. Addictions provide this for some.

As we recover our sense of joy, we will be able to take pleasure in the ordinary. Walking in the rain, skipping stones across water or watching sandpipers play tag with the surf becomes a time of wonder.

Joy is an attitude which is ours to experience when we choose to.

Today I will choose joy as an attitude.

FEBRUARY 20

May the outward and inward man be as one.

Socrates

What Socrates said centuries ago is the fulcrum on which recovery turns. When we learn to match our behavior with corresponding emotions, we are whole.

Early on in life, the disease of alcoholism threw a monkey wrench into our emotional machinery and it stopped. Not having the skill to repair it properly, we got it running in fits and starts, using a small make-believe tool set — the only tools available to a child. In the struggle to keep the machinery running with one hand, and being pulled into the conflict with the other, we parted company with our genuine emotions and learned to behave whatever way it took to survive.

With the grown-up tools of recovery we can synchronize our emotions and behavior and have them work as a unit.

I can learn to express my feelings honestly and directly.

FEBRUARY 21

We boil at different degrees.

Ralph Waldo Emerson

Anger is a major problem for co-dependents. Some of us boil at the freezing point and some of us freeze at the boiling point.

Identifying anger and using it appropriately is something we didn't learn as children. We were preoccupied with trying to maneuver through the minefield in our homes.

We need to understand why we substitute anger for hurt, or why anger turns into self-hate or self-pity, or why we think we are terrible people if we feel this forbidden emotion.

I am relearning attitudes about anger. I can learn to express it appropriately.

Adversity has the effect of eliciting talents which in prosperous circumstances would have lain dormant.

Horace

If we had three wishes, they would be that our childhood had been blue skies, sunshine and fluffy clouds. But wishing will never make it so. The next best thing we can do is look for the silver lining in the turbulent clouds of our co-dependent past. In that silver lining we will discover a marvelous array of gifts that were bestowed upon us as we survived our adversity.

In whatever role we took to cope, we acquired valuable skills and keen instincts, developing a high degree of compassion and sensitivity. We learned to deal with crises that would bring giants to their knees.

I will learn to see, appreciate and use the talents I developed as a child.

FEBRUARY 23

God has put something noble and good into every heart which His hand created.

Mark Twain

When we were born, we were spiritually intact. Tucked somewhere between a bald head and tiny toes was everything we needed to be a whole human being. In the difficulty of growing up, this special part of us broke into two pieces. We call them guilt and shame. This is what we bring with us to adulthood.

But in our brokenness we berate and abuse ourselves unmercifully.

Imagine an antique doll, her hair in clumps, a chip in her nose, her gown in musty tatters. Once perfect, now a relic found in an old trunk. But look again. All that she was is still there in the haunting stare of her eyes. She is waiting to be lifted and made whole again.

I am reclaiming my wholeness and my spirituality.

FEBRUARY 24

The lowest ebb is the turn of the tide.

Henry Wadsworth Longfellow

To heal is to reach into the depths of ourselves and bring to the surface feelings that have been denied. The numbness and fear felt before beginning the process of recovery served as deflectors, keeping deep hurts from emerging. But when those hurts make themselves known, the pain of loss can be intense. This is our lowest ebb.

Out of this grief comes our salvation, our serenity and our spirituality. We emerge from our depths free of the pull of our past. Free of the denial we were drowning in. Free to flow toward our horizons.

I emerge from my grief to find serenity.

We are children of our landscape.

Lawrence Durrell

The landscape of our childhood was wobbly. Our parents changed color without warning, and what was true one moment was not true the next. We learned to hide, to duck and to pretend.

And as adults we have incorporated that landscape into our emotional lives. Our emotions are wobbly, they change color, seemingly without reason. The truth — how we feel about ourselves — varies from moment to moment.

We can change this landscape, create an emotional world of rolling hills and gentle valleys lush with life.

To make it come true is to believe that it can.

I can't change my past but I can change my emotional world and find happiness.

FEBRUARY 26

Even God can't start a parked car.

Many of us have read volumes of books, gone to every workshop and conference available and attend 12-Step meetings on a regular basis. We *know* what the problem is. But knowing isn't doing. Knowing is having the information in our heads, and *doing* is transferring the problem to our hearts where the real healing takes place.

This is not to imply that going from information-gathering to action is easy. If it were easy — given how miserable we feel — we would have taken action long ago. Healing isn't something that can be learned, it has to be felt. Twelve-Step programs provide us with the key. But *we* have to turn the engine on and provide the fuel — to get going down the road to recovery.

With the help of a power greater than myself I can find the courage to recover.

Stay humble or stumble.

To be humble is to be balanced in our opinion of ourselves. Humility does not swagger with false pride nor grovel in self-depreciation. Humility is accepting the truth about ourselves.

The good news for co-dependents and adult children is that we are blessed with many fine qualities that we have negated. We need to stand tall and be grateful for these gifts. "Thank you" should become a part of our emotional vocabulary.

False pride is often a stance taken to cover up terrible feelings of inadequacy.

But the truth is we have our own unique worth.

Today I will accept my good qualities and acknowledge my defects. I have the courage to change my behavior and the wisdom to change my false beliefs.

FEBRUARY 28

He ain't heavy, he's my brother.

Father Flanagan

When we attend our first 12-Step meeting, most of us feel that we've finally found a home, a family of people we don't have to pretend with, be afraid of, feel inferior to. A family of people who understand and accept us. And oh, how good it feels!

In this new home, our brothers and sisters hold us up until we can stand alone. They show us compassion and help us through our grief. We discover we are a blessing not a burden to our new family. We are allowing them to give the very best of themselves and in doing so, they grow in serenity and spirituality. We learn that to give and to receive is the same act of love.

In my new family I am loved.

MARCH 1

Regret to human beings is what mud is to hogs — it's good only for wallowing in.

A short wallow in the mud hole of regret may be a cleansing thing for humans. Regret makes us feel bad, makes us take a good look at ourselves, clean up our act. But to stay there indefinitely is as fatal to our recovery as butchering day!

Regret draws us to the mud hole and often guilt keeps us firmly entrenched. And there we sit, stuck in the mire, not knowing how to crawl out.

Fortunately, there is a way out — just open our mouths and squeal, "God! Help me! I'm stuck!"

Regret and guilt bog me down. With help from a Higher Power I pull myself free and get on with the business of recovery.

MARCH 2

If I am not for myself, who will be?

The Talmud

In recovery we can begin to care for ourselves again. Begin to look after our own best interest, speak up on our own behalf, stand up and be counted.

Until we reach that point in healing, there are things we can do to encourage the emergence of our authentic child. When the old negative tapes start to whirl in our heads, we can drown them out with positive affirmations. We can begin to act "as if" we already believe in our self-worth. And we can accept the genuine love and support of others who have traveled this same journey of rediscovery.

I am a worthy human being created by the hands of a Higher Power. I have a right and an obligation to be all that I can be.

MARCH 3

There are many tears in the heart that never reach the eyes.

Tears are a way of expressing sadness and loss. They are meant to flow from us. When they are trapped in deep pockets inside our hearts, they form a pool and weigh us down.

If we do not grieve our losses openly, above ground, then sadness will seep underground and surface as another emotion. We may become angry, cynical or physically ill. Or we may hang emotionally suspended, like a waterfall stalled in midair.

Recovery is the process of opening the flood gates that block the free flow of tears. We will not drown in sorrow. Instead we will be bathed in the clear waters of healing.

I will let the tears of loss flow from my heart. My Higher Power will not give me more than I can handle as I work through my grief.

MARCH 4

Never get into a squirting match with a skunk!

A lot of polecats roam around parading as people and the sooner we spot them, the better. They have us out-weaponed with cunning and deception, and unless we're willing to squirt back the same noxious potion, we'd better make tracks.

The sooner we stop trying to save every stray critter armed with teeth or fangs or stingers or sacs with vile-smelling juice, the easier it will be for us to get on with our own lives. When these unhappy creatures genuinely want our help, they will come to us, defenses down. Then when we reach out, we can be reasonably sure that we won't get bit, stung or sprayed for our efforts.

The only responsibility I have when being manipulated by someone is to protect myself.

MARCH 5

Nothing comes from nothing.

Some children are born into lives so void of nurturing that they do not survive, but good things happened to most of us as children and they were delicious. Within our families there were days or perhaps weeks of relative sanity and continuity where we felt loved and out of harm's way — for the moment at least. In these precious hours, we had not the lion's share, but at least some happiness. And most of us had someone — an aunt, a teacher, a neighbor — who served as an anchor in the storm.

Today I am grateful for any good times in my past and for those who were there for me when I needed someone.

MARCH 6

To err is human; to cover it up is more human.

To make mistakes is part of being human. But when co-dependents pull even a minor faux pas, we beat ourselves over the head with it and announce to the world that we are miserable failures.

This tendency toward self-abuse stems from the legacy of shame and guilt that is handed down in dysfunctional families. We felt that the problems in our homes were somehow our fault, and we carried that sense of guilt with us into adulthood. Now when something goes wrong within a hundred mile radius of us, we automatically take the blame.

Recovery lifts the weight of the world from our shoulders. We stop taking responsibility for past and present things that are not our fault, and we stop being so hard on ourselves when we are at fault.

I am human and entitled to my share of mistakes and errors.

MARCH 7

A joy shared is a joy made double.

English proverb

To watch the unabashed joy of a baby clanging pots and pans or laughing at the surprise of a peek-a-boo make most adults weak in the knees with shared joy. Once-upon-a-time we were that free and alive, and it is a vicarious thrill to again be in touch with that glorious child within us.

In recovery we share our pain and as we work through our losses, we are grateful to be able to give and receive the precious gift of joy.

Joy! It is mine to give and to receive.

A young Trooper should have an old Horse.

Thomas Fuller

A newcomer to Co-dependents Anonymous (CoDA) groups would be wise to saddle up to an old-timer who knows the trail well — someone who knows when to take it slow and easy, when to gallop and knows how to stop dead in his tracks when he hears the command, "Whoa!" This old-timer leads until the greenhorn can handle the reins without going around in circles.

Newcomers are often raring to go, but they don't know where. They take off in any direction only to run into hurdles, or trip into holes. Others may never get out of the stable if they're not guided through those first critical steps.

When I need direction, I will ask someone who knows the way.

MARCH 9

Being entirely honest with oneself is a good exercise.

Sigmund Freud

We can jog ourselves to fitness, but we have to *honest* ourselves to recovery. And this is harder work than jogging. We have contorted ourselves out of shape with dishonesty and denial, and it will require discipline and dedication to reshape the truth of our feelings and behavior.

Twelve-Step programs offer a work-out guaranteed to bring out the best in us. We need only apply the principles on a daily basis. And when we need a second wind, get on our knees and pray.

I can break through denial and discover the truth about myself. That truth will set me free.

MARCH 10

The best place to find a helping hand is at the end of your arm.

Being helpless is a powerful ploy. With it we can keep others in bondage to our needs. We can manipulate and control them by appealing to their desire to be helpful and their sense of guilt. They will resent us for taking advantage of their good intentions, and when two people are stuck in co-dependent relationships, neither one is looking out for his well-being in a healthy manner.

Self-preservation means to use our hands, our heads and our hearts to help ourselves. When we can do this, then the give and take of healthy relationships will find its rhythm.

I choose to be self-reliant when I can, but ask for help when I genuinely need it.

MARCH 11

Wisely and Slowly: They stumble that run fast.

Shakespeare

"Run for your life! But watch where you're going."

Recovery *is* a run for our lives. And as such, great care should be taken not to run into brick walls or trip from hurrying in the dark.

To retrace the steps of our past is exacting work. It requires patience and perseverance. And it takes wisdom to know what to do with the emergence of our authentic selves. It is not wise to burn bridges as we begin to make changes in our lives.

There is no fast lane on the road to recovery. It is traveled one step at a time.

With the help of my Higher Power I will be patient in my recovery and wise in my decisions.

MARCH 12

After a while you learn the subtle difference between holding a hand and chaining a soul.

Kara DiGiovanna

The families we grew up in could be likened to a tangle of vines entwined so tightly, it became impossible to separate them. In this unhealthy garden we did not receive adequate nourishment and light to grow to maturity. We learned only to cling or be clung to for our survival. This choking off of self is at the root of co-dependency.

We enter adulthood feeling incomplete. We send off shoots and begin to twist around one another. Without recovery we will spend our lives clinging and being clung to as we did in childhood.

I no longer want to tower over nor cower beneath others. I want to stand beside them.

MARCH 13

Natural forces within us are the true healers of disease.

Hippocrates

As medical science discovers more and more about the human body it is apparent that Hippocrates, a man who lived 400 years before Christ, knew what he was talking about. He treated his patients with proper diet, fresh air, attention to habits and living conditions, and minimized the use of drugs.

We now know that our bodies produce a myriad of chemicals, hormones and enzymes that can help us to heal both physical and mental maladies. The more we learn about the complexity of the human body, the more we marvel at the wonder of it.

When we apply Hippocrates' treatment of healthy habits, and work the 12 Steps, we are placing ourselves in a condition that allows the natural forces within us to perform their miracles.

My body and mind have within them the power to heal me. And with the help of my Creator, I can be healthy and whole.

MARCH 14

We are always getting ready to live but never living.

Ralph Waldo Emerson

"When I lose 40 pounds, I'll be happy." "Next year I'll take an art class." "One of these days . . ."

Many of us hang around the starting gate of life, but never go around the track. We have plans and fully intend to carry them out . . . when conditions are right.

Fear, laziness or not knowing how to begin, are a few reasons we hold back from pursuing goals or following dreams. Or we take a negative stance and say no to life.

Each day is a gift. We can squander it or make it splendid. It's our choice.

I will live today to its fullest. I will take action and make plans for pursuing my goals and dreams.

MARCH 15

Always behave like a duck — keep calm and unruffled on the surface but paddle like the devil underneath.

Jacob Braude

People from dysfunctional homes paddle around in denial most of the time. We are expert at tucking fear under our wings. As youngsters this behavior saved our tail-feathers and became an automatic response to life. The problem *now* is that we don't trust anything in the pond, and don't know in which direction to paddle. So we kick around in a small lonely circle . . . pretending.

Healing is to ruffle those stiff feathers, make them pliable enough to touch the soft down of vulnerability buried beneath. And in this touching, we will learn how to glide serenely and skillfully over the full expanse of our pond.

I am learning to trust and to feel. I am moving toward the clear waters of serenity.

MARCH 16

Not tonight, I have a headache.

Multitudes

If the truth were told, this age-old excuse would go: "Not tonight, you hurt my feelings." "Not tonight, I am afraid." "Not tonight, I think sex is bad." "Not tonight, I'm getting even." "Not tonight, I have a heartache."

When we are brought up in homes where sexuality is displayed in unhealthy patterns, our developing sexual selves become distorted. And if we were molested as children, this makes the task of becoming healthy sexual beings even more difficult.

Sexuality has to do with sensitivity, spirituality, passion and compassion. As we recover from the wounds of our past, the fear and confusion plaguing us about sex will be clarified. With these insights we can begin to find joy and honesty in all aspects of our sexuality.

I am spirit, mind and body. Sexuality is part of all that I am. I will treat all aspects of myself with respect and honesty.

MARCH 17

Tears are for important things.

Adult Child

Tears are a physical response, as well as an emotional response to feelings. Some Adult Children's tears are so dammed up that a trickle can't leak through, while others have tears that run like a leaky faucet needing new washers. Either way, we are in need of repair.

In recovery we will learn to cry for important things — like the loss of our childhood. And we will learn not to cry just because we don't know what else to do about how we feel. We will be able to respond in a healthy appropriate way to the events in our lives.

I will learn to respect the importance of tears. I will learn to cry for myself.

It's all in the way you look at it. A flea is delighted to learn that her children are going to the dogs.

Ctenocephalides Canis

There are few real truths in life and even these are debatable. Our beliefs are what give our world — inner and outer — its reality. Some people go to the "dog-mas" and adhere righteously to a one-and-only truth that allows little room for the beliefs of others. Sadly they can't enjoy the wide view that is open to us all.

As our own self-respect grows in recovery, we will be able to express our views about life and will not be uncomfortable when our opinions differ from our neighbor's. And we will be enriched by learning from, and being tolerant of, the beliefs of others.

I will be tolerant and respectful of the beliefs of others.

If you can't receive, then giving becomes manipulation.

L.A. Law (TV series)

This is a harsh thought, but there is much truth in it. The one thing that many co-dependents hold on to as being worthwhile in themselves is generosity. So why knock holes in the one attribute we feel good about? Because in this generosity of spirit, we forgot somebody. Ourselves!

Until we can receive the love others offer us, and until we can love ourselves, much of the generosity we offer is tainted with the need for approval and the need for control. And in this state of manipulation it is difficult to sort out which generosities are unselfish and which ones are motivated by our unhealthy needs.

I will give myself the same generosity I give to others, and I will learn the difference between manipulation and genuine giving.

MARCH 20

Courage is resistance to fear, mastery of fear, not absence of fear.

Mark Twain

Co-dependents are riddled with fear. But we don't always know what we are afraid of. So we walk around with our guards up, carrying a free-floating fear that jumps from shadows, imagined things and people at large.

Recovery is to tame that fear, give it a name and a face so we can confront it, rather than cowering before its might. We are David. It is Goliath; the giant of our childhood who stomped down hard on all that we were, who flattened and distorted our emotions until we knew only shame, guilt and fear.

I am gaining the courage to face and conquer my fear.

MARCH 21

Spring is God's way of saying, "One more time!"

For adult children winter was harsh and long. We remained frozen beneath the surface as the cycle of life repeated itself. In the warming of springtime, when the vibrations of life moved around us, we pushed small shoots of growth through to the surface, but without healthy roots to sustain the unfolding, we were stunted and not able to blossom.

And then a miracle. Nurtured by understanding, coaxed by loving hands, we push through from our frozen world and thrive. Each season we grow stronger, straighter, and we open to become the beautiful creation that we were always meant to be.

I welcome spring. Today I grow stronger.

MARCH 22

If you don't know where you are going, you may miss it when you get there.

If we think that recovery means happy-ever-after, we are in need of new directions.

In recovery we still have to deal with the reality of being human and all that it entails. We will still hurt, be frightened, get frustrated, feel lost, be lonely and experience the frailty and vulnerability that all people feel. But it will be balanced with a sense of confidence that we can solve and overcome our problems and difficulties. Recovery is the road to healthy living and loving. And that is enough to make the journey through life worth the effort.

I am not looking for a life free from pain and problems. I am looking for the wisdom and serenity to deal with life effectively and find a measure of happiness and contentment.

MARCH 23

The milk of human kindness beats cold cream for wrinkles.

They say that we have the face we deserve by the time we are 40. If we have dipped from jars of resentment and bitterness over the years, our faces reflect those emotions with tell-tale signs. A furrowed brow, narrowed eyes and clenched teeth signal our mistrust and hostility. When the love in our hearts is blocked, our eyes appear like cold marbles, void of life.

At any point in life we can begin to apply healing lotions to our negative attitudes and stop the damage being done to our physical and spiritual selves. The choice is ours. When we have found serenity, our faces soften, our eyes glow with warmth and our hearts are open to kindness and love.

I will let go of resentments and bitterness. These negative emotions are standing in the way of kindness and recovery.

MARCH 24

The truth shall set you free, but at first it will make you miserable.

Garfield

For the co-dependent there is no more sobering thought than this. To begin the process of recovery it is necessary to come out of a state of suspended emotion. To discover the truth of ourselves we have to open old wounds and bleed. We have to inflict pain on ourselves.

Out of this self-imposed pain we rediscover our authentic self — a precious child held in bondage, longing to be free. We allow that child to express pent-up feelings, allow that child to cry and allow that child to emerge into the bright light of truth. When our misery is spent, the child within and the adult are one.

With the help of a power greater than myself and the support of others, I can face the pain of my past.

MARCH 25

A barber asked King Archelaus how he would like his hair cut. "In silence," replied the king.

Archelaus

Silence gives us the opportunity to speak with ourselves. Inner dialogue is an intimate visit with the most important person in our lives. If we don't know what we are about, we won't be able to discern accurately what others are about.

Silence is frightening for many of us. We are uneasy when alone and seek noise and distraction to block out the inner quiet. In doing so, we lose the richest part of ourselves.

In recovery we learn to be alone with our thoughts to discover that in the serene silence of our hearts and minds is the essence of humanity, humility and love.

Today I will be at ease with silence. I will listen quietly to my inner voice.

MARCH 26

I enjoy being spontaneous — whenever it is appropriate.

From Cheers (TV Series)

One of the glaring telltale signs of co-dependents are the constraints we put on all of our feelings — and that includes spontaneous enjoyment. It was never safe to express feelings, so we learned to stifle them. We got so good at covering them up that we all but forgot what they were.

Learning to let inner feelings tumble out in healthy abandon is one of the tasks of recovery. At first we can only playact at spontaneity. That's all right, it's a beginning. And when that first unconstrained "something" sneaks out, be it laughter or tears, we may feel embarrassed and uncomfortable. And that's all right, too. We are in the process of learning to be our natural selves. Wow!

My natural self is spontaneous. Today I will enjoy being me.

MARCH 27

Be not afraid of growing slowly, be afraid only of standing still.

Two seeds beneath the ground felt the warmth above them and knew it was time. They pushed up through the earth and began to reach toward the great blue sky. Soon buds appeared on both plants. One bud opened slightly, looked around and was afraid. It pulled back into itself and hung its head, destined always to grow in the shade.

A bud on the other plant, curious to see over the tall grasses, stretched as tall as it could and felt a warm glow on its face. The bud was so enthralled by the warm light that it stretched even taller to watch the sun until it disappeared into the sea.

The sunflower was so busy stretching to see that it didn't notice that it had grown taller than all the other flowers.

I want to grow and become all that God intended me to be.

MARCH 28

When a man is wrapped up in himself, he makes a pretty small package.

John Ruskin

Selfish people are like misers, hoarding more than they need, depriving others of an equal share. But even after they have lined their shelves with excesses, they come up bare.

Selfishness stems from fear and is an attempt to fill up loneliness. When we aren't able to truly love or be loved, we are compelled to fill our emptiness with something. In quiet desperation, we elbow our way through life, demanding to be first in whatever line we are standing in.

The tools of recovery show us how to rearrange the shelves of our hearts to make room for love.

When I give up being selfish, I give up being lonely and fearful. When I let others in, I let myself out of the small world I am trapped in.

MARCH 29

If you don't throw it, they can't hit it.

Lefty Gomez

When we drop out of the co-dependent game, the other player is left at home plate, the bat readied for a pitch. But it doesn't come. The game is over for one of the players in an unhealthy relationship. This is an ending — the ninth inning — but it can be a beginning if the other player is willing to make it so.

As we recover, we stop being a part of the win-or-lose cycle of co-dependency. If our partners choose to pursue in the old game, and it undermines our efforts at being independent adults, we may have to break with those persons. When we are able to take our own stance in life, we're batting 400!

I am responsible for myself. I will not let co-dependency interfere with my recovery and serenity. If my partner isn't ready or willing to heal, I can pull away with love.

MARCH 30

All looks yellow to a jaundiced eye.

Alexander Pope

To feel fleeting moments of envy is human. It goes away with the blink of an eye. But when we look out from behind eyes that are filled with resentment and envy, our world becomes discolored and lonely. With clouded vision we are doomed to walk into trees, fall into ruts and wander down dead-end trails in search of something on which to pin our unhappiness.

To lug a backpack of envy bogs us down and saps our energy. We need to sit down on the hard rock called Truth and unload our pack of negative attitudes. Only then will we be able to come out of the woods to see how blue the sky is.

Envy is a barrier to my happiness. I am learning to be grateful for what I have, and gracious toward the good fortune of others.

MARCH 31

If I die, I forgive you. If I recover, we shall see.

Spanish proverb

Forgiveness can come in stages. Most of us work toward it a step at a time. Maybe tentative attempts are the best we can do at first. We aren't yet ready or able to give up the anger and resentment that keeps others who have hurt us at a distance. Perhaps loving is too painful for now. Others may experience thunderbolt healings and forgive with the wave of a wand. Everyone has their own pace, their own way of patching up their wounds. It is not up to anyone else to judge another's mode of recovery.

Forgiveness is the entrance to spirituality. It is a hard door to open for some. The task of those who have already gone through that door is to help soothe the fears and doubts of those who hesitate to enter into love.

When I am able to forgive, I will find happiness, love and spirituality.

APRIL 1

Change favors the prepared mind.

Louis Pasteur

Thank God and the hard work of dedicated professionals, we now have knowledge and understanding of the problems that confront those of us who have grown up in dysfunctional homes. This knowledge gives us the tools we need to begin healing.

This gathering of knowledge should not become a substitute for "the real thing." Healing comes from working through painful emotions of loss. Preparation for the battle begins in our mind, but it is fought and won in our hearts — the birthplace of change.

With a prepared mind and willing heart I will recover.

APRIL 2

When the cat and mouse agree, the grocer is ruined.

Persian proverb

When one of the participants of the "chase or be chased" game of co-dependency decides to call it quits, the other is left to chase after its own tail. Hopefully, the confused participant will wise up and head in a direction that will lead somewhere.

When both parties let go of the behaviors and attitudes that keeps them tethered in an unhealthy relationship, the destructive game is over. They are free to grow as individuals and free to participate in a healthy, interdependent relationship.

Co-dependency blocks my happiness and growth. I can learn to function as an independent adult.

APRIL 3

There's nothing more irritating than a savior when you aren't ready to be saved.

D. Sutton

"I have good news! I know what's wrong with you and how to fix it! In just 12 easy steps . . ." What will happen here is that The Savee will back off 12 giant steps from the onslaught of this crusader, The Savior.

When we are too zealous in our approach to those we feel could benefit from what we know as informed co-dependents, we scare them off. We are asking them to give up a belief system that has allowed them to survive. We are asking them to turn themselves inside out because we think it will be good for them.

If by our example, our growth, they ask, "How?" then we can offer a gentle nudging, a sensitive suggestion, rather than pushing them from behind.

I will be sensitive to the fears of others who have not begun to heal from the wounds of their childhood.

APRIL 4

You can't eat your friends and have them, too.
Budd Schulberg

Some co-dependent people go around like Pac-man, gobbling up everything that crosses their paths as they rush around this maze called life. Smiling, they gobble up all the problems, decide on all the solutions, tell others how things should be done, then do it for them. They take on the world single-mouthed and don't give others the opportunity to learn, to make mistakes or to do things a different way. In their need for control, they eliminate the reality of other people. And they do this in the name of love.

But thy name is not Love. It is Control. It is Co-dependency. It is the mishmash left over from our contorted childhood.

In recovery we are grateful to be able to close our mouths, open our hands and let go.

Today I will not tell the sun when to rise or set.

APRIL 5

Here's to the past. Thank God, it's past!

That's the good news. The bad news is that it takes more than a toast to break free of the past.

Recovery does not leap from A to Z as we might like it to. We cannot skirt around it and hope to find genuine serenity. There's only one way out, and that is to tiptoe, stomp, march and sometimes dance right through the middle of it. It is a simple one, two, three step. Simple but it requires pain, patience and persistence.

And the good news is that we don't have to do it alone. We have a host of people who have learned the steps and are there to help see us through.

If I persist, have patience, feel my feelings, I can be free from the pain of my past.

APRIL 6

Living is like licking honey off a thorn.

This is an apt introduction to life. There are times when life is a beautiful garden, sweet with the fragrance of living and loving. And there are times when life jabs like thorns, makes us pull back and bleed. The art of living is to drink the sweetness and heal from the wounds.

Our attitude determines if roses have thorns, or if thorns have roses. And the degree to which we are willing to risk and grow determines the lushness of our life.

The promise of recovery is that life will have more roses and less thorns than before.

I am learning to smell the roses and heal from the wounds of the past.

APRIL 7

No call alligator long mouth till you pass him.

Jamaican proverb

Occasionally people are called upon in emergencies to act without forethought to save another from injury or death. This kind of courage comes partly from our bodies' physiological response to crisis; large amounts of adrenalin turn us into "super" men and women until the crisis is over.

In less traumatic circumstances, courage is a quiet, thoughtful, deliberate way of being or behaving. We act out of conviction or sometimes nagging doubt, take a giant step and hope for the best. This is the kind of courage it takes to make changes in our lives.

I pray for the courage and wisdom to make changes in my life.

APRIL 8

He is a true friend. He stabs you in the front.
Leonard Louis Levinson

Twelve-Step programs are about friendship. The kind that cuts through deception and denial. Our honesty with each other is a frontal attack on the shields we hold to protect the unhealed wounds of childhood — wounds that need the air and light of truth to heal.

The friendships formed in support groups run deep. They are borne of empathy and trust. Our friends look past our defenses into our hearts. With their love and honesty we can put down our shields and come out into the open.

My true friends are honest with me because they have been honest with themselves.

APRIL 9

The game of life is not so much in holding a good hand as playing a poor hand well.

H. T. Leslie

To heal is to look at the cards we were dealt as children, throw away what is useless, and build on what will help us win. It's a long drawn-out game and the stakes are high. We're in it for our lives.

Gratefully, in this game — this second chance — the deck is stacked in our favor and we are the dealers, using a new deck of cards. With help from the skilled hands of a Higher Power, we can't lose.

I can choose what to keep and what to throw away from my past, and can turn my losses into gains.

APRIL 10

Let the past drift away with the water.

Japanese saying

The waters of our co-dependent childhood were troubled. Churning water hissed and hurled, swallowing us in a frenzy of crises. Much of the quiet times between crises we stagnated in murky pools of confusion and denial. As adults we still shudder at the hissing water, and our emotions remain trapped in those murky pools.

Recovery is finding a way out and flowing toward the river. As we bump over rocky places, tumble down falls and drink in sunlight, we are purified with new life.

Slowly I am letting go of my past. I am finding my way toward health, happiness and spirituality.

APRIL 11

He who would leap high must take a long run.

Danish proverb

The co-dependent's run through childhood was like an obstacle course. Hurdles bigger than life loomed ahead, too big to even climb over, much less jump over. And often we were weighed down lugging responsibilities far beyond our abilities. Somehow, we managed to stumble over the line to adulthood with a gasp.

That grueling race provided us with muscle and stamina. Recovery coaches us in how to put our skills to their best uses, and how to let go of habits that slow us down. When we get our second wind in recovery, we are on our way to becoming winners!

I have what it takes to grow and leap high in life. I need only to believe in myself to make it happen.

APRIL 12

The course of true anything never does run smooth.

Samuel Butler

Like being in love, the course of recovery has its peaks and valleys. We can go from elation to despair in a heartbeat. Frustrated, we want to throw the diamond back and shout, "The engagement is off! We're through!"

But, alas, once we have started down the aisle of recovery there is no turning back without paying a price. We have committed to a union of two souls — our adult selves and the lost child that waits within.

As long as I remain willing and open to change, recovery will be mine.

APRIL 13

Whatever you may be sure of, be sure of this — that you are dreadfully like other people.

James Russell Lowell

One of the first healings that happen to newcomers to 12-Step programs is the realization that they are not alone. They see mirror images of their inner selves looking back with compassion and understanding. And what a relief it is to discover that there are other people like them.

This is the first step away from isolation, the first step toward connecting with others. Our miserable "uniqueness" gives way to feelings of kinship with people who have traveled the same disjointed road into adulthood.

I am not alone. I am not different. I am a human who needs to heal from the wounds of my childhood. I am part of a large family who knows who I am and cares.

APRIL 14

The best armor is to keep out of range.

Italian proverb

In the rebirth of recovery we may at first be as wobbly as newborn colts. Alive, eager to try our first steps, we do well when surrounded by others from the same meadow. But put us back in the pasture with those of our family who have not begun the process of healing, and our spindly legs might buckle under us.

Early on in healing it might be well to keep distance between ourselves and those who can still knock us down. We have gained strength, but not enough to withstand the stampede of conflicting behavior that comes at us from our dysfunctional families. Until our legs are stronger, and we know our way back to the meadow, to back off can be a step in the right direction.

I will surround myself with people who help me to grow, and will protect myself from those who hamper my progress.

APRIL 15

Find the grain of truth in criticism — chew it and swallow it.

D. Sutton

Criticism stings. Even a well-intended comment that could be helpful, makes some of us cower in trepidation and others of us glower with retaliation. These are involuntary responses. What we do with criticism after that is a choice.

If we hear the same criticism from an assortment of people, perhaps there is a grain of truth in it. It might benefit us to sit down and mull it around with open minds.

Petty, mean and ignorant people abound in this world, and their criticisms aren't worth a tinker's dam. But the observations and insights from people who have our well-being at heart may be worthy of consideration.

I can benefit from positive criticism and can recover from the stings of negative people.

APRIL 16

He sheltered from the rain under the drainpipe.

Persian proverb

Addictions are a way to protect ourselves from the feelings dammed up inside us. And indeed they temporarily dampen emotion and reality. So we crouch under the drainpipe of addiction, alone in a puddle of despair, ignoring the fact that we are drowning.

Recovery begins when we crawl out, lift our face and arms to the sky, and sputter our finest prayer: "God help me, I'm all wet!"

Addictions keep me from feeling and from healing. I want to be healthy and happy. With the help of a Higher Power I will find serenity.

APRIL 17

I got a simple rule about everybody. If you don't treat me right — shame on you.

Louis Armstrong

Like gallant gentlemen of old, many co-dependents go around throwing cloaks over puddles while sloshing up to the knees in water, only to catch cold. We treat others well, while neglecting ourselves.

This servitude is triggered by our fragile self-esteem and our bottomless need for approval — at any cost. As we go back and gather the parts of ourselves left behind in childhood, we can piece ourselves together into a whole person — one deserving of respect, from ourselves and from others.

I am learning to treat myself with the same respect that I treat others. This is my right and my obligation.

APRIL 18

Today if you're not confused, you're just not thinking clearly.

Irene Peter

Newcomers (and not-so-newcomers) sometimes lament, "I'm confused!" They feel that something is wrong or that they are going backward in recovery. This ain't necessarily so. Often confusion is a pile of linen in need of sorting.

Until we begin the process of healing, denial tosses our emotions in dark corners. As we begin to sort through and launder this musty heap, it is no wonder that we get confused!

Recovery takes work. Some of the wrinkles of our past are harder to iron out than others. Perhaps we aren't yet willing to discard old behaviors, or are afraid to try new ones. Denial and reality fold over each other and we are baffled.

When I am confused, I have the opportunity to grow or have an excuse to stay where I am.

APRIL 19

Without forgiveness life is governed by . . . an endless cycle of resentment and retaliation.

Roberto Assagioli

Forgiveness has two layers. The upper layer is of the mind and intellect: We understand, therefore we forgive. The matter is tucked away in the folds of our memories and considered finished business. But in our haste to mend, we didn't knot the thread, forgiveness pulls loose and resentment frays our composure.

The second layer of forgiveness is of the heart. To get to it requires that we reach into the depths of ourselves and sort through the tatters of emotion that await our unfolding. When we have completed our task, forgiveness drapes, soft and warm, around our hearts.

When I can fully forgive, I will find serenity.

APRIL 20

The best way to know God is to love many things.

Vincent Van Gogh

This issue of God, a Higher Power or whatever "IT" is called, is a knotty problem for many co-dependents. The abandonment we felt as children left us wary and mistrusting of a heavenly father. Life on earth felt more like hell than heaven. So we enter adulthood cynical and negative about matters of the spirit.

When we are caught in the dilemma of *wanting* to believe but not being able to digest the buzz words, it may help to think of God as whatever it is that touches our inner self.

Perhaps it's love of children or animals, appreciation of nature. Maybe it's admiration of creativity or respect for benevolent intelligence. Or it may be that first sigh of relief when we found the support and understanding of other co-dependents.

As I recover from the abandonment of my past, I will begin to rediscover my spirituality.

APRIL 21

Humility is to make a right estimate of one's self.
Charles Haddon Spurgeon

To strut with conceit about being chosen as "Miss Kumquat" is narcissistic pride. To feel superior and arrogant because we can afford to wear a Rolex watch is boastful pride. Both attitudes are negative. But to be proud of a painting we've dabbled with for hours to get just right or pleased to be given a promotion for good work at the office are positive feelings. We have put our best efforts into something we value, and our reward is an inner sense of well-being.

As for humility, if it is worn as a badge of honor, we have pinned it on backward. True humility comes from being grateful for our good fortune and talents and aware of our flaws and shortcomings.

In recovery, humility and pride will take their proper place in my heart.

APRIL 22

Don't think there are no crocodiles because the water is calm.

Malaysian proverb

Like a predator lurking deep beneath the surface, our denied feeling lies in wait, and when it lashes its tail and sinks its teeth deep into us, our pain receptors go numb.

Denial protected us when we were young, but the longer we continue to use it as adults, the more wounded we will be. Many of us search for help in the wrong places (addictions and unhealthy relationships) and suffer more injury.

Healing begins when we face what we believe is "the enemy." Feelings are our allies; when we work *with* them, instead of *against* them, we are on our way to wellness.

I can no longer find refuge in denial, addictions or co-dependent behavior. I pray for the courage to face my fears and change.

APRIL 23

Never grow a wishbone, daughter, where your backbone ought to be.

Clementine Paddleford

One of the first things we learn about recovery is that it is not for the faint-hearted. Healing is a matter of blood, sweat and tears. There is no short-cut, no easy way out.

When we see others who are further along in the healing process, we wish that we could have the serenity they have — now, and without the hard work involved. We hope that perhaps if we get close enough, some of it will rub off on us.

When we give up *wishing* for recovery and start *working* at recovery, it will be ours, a step at a time.

I cannot wish myself to wholeness, I must work my way there.

APRIL 24

If you have built castles in the air, your work need not be lost; that is where they should be. Now put the foundation under them.

Henry David Thoreau

If long after childhood we are still dreaming of being rescued by a knight in shining armor, or turning from a frog to a handsome prince when kissed by a princess, we are bound to be let down by life. But if our dreams are for love, intimacy, peace of mind, and self-esteem, we are longing for things that are within our reach.

When we begin to believe in ourselves, we can build the solid foundation needed to pursue our goals and make our dreams come true.

My dreams of wholeness and happiness are within my reach.

APRIL 25

Never eat anything at one sitting that you can't lift.

Miss Piggy

In our hunger to recover, many co-dependents take on too much at once. We heap our plates with issues and dig in with a shovel. It is no wonder that after this gluttonous attack we are weighed down with fatigue and sour with heartburn.

The issues that we face are heavy with pain. We need to deal with them in small portions so they won't consume us. And we need to allow time between bites to savor the sweet morsels of recovery.

I will not take on more than I can handle, and I am grateful for the recovery I am gaining day by day.

APRIL 26

He who masters the grey everyday is a hero.

Fyodor Dostoyevsky

Grey is a state of mind that blots out the possibilities an ordinary day may hold. We discover that the ordinary can become extraordinary if viewed from a different slant, just as dust motes floating in a stream of sunlight take on a beauty all their own.

To conquer the boredom of everyday we need to change our attitudes about what excitement is. How will we be able to expand our interests if we don't try something new — like gardening? To our surprise we may be thrilled enough to want to send out birth announcements when the first tomato appears.

Today I will look with new eyes at the ordinary things in my life.

APRIL 27

Life's a pretty precious and wonderful thing. You can't sit down and let it lap around you. You have to plunge into it; you have to dive through it.

Kyle Crichton

Some people are content to sit on the shore of life and watch. Content may not be the word, perhaps they have resigned themselves, for whatever reason, to being observers. And there are others who would like to take the plunge but are afraid.

Those in recovery took the plunge and are overcoming fear. We know what we are missing by being detached, and are weary of being caught in the currents of other people's lives. Our wish is to be free of the pull of the past so that we can ebb and flow in rhythm with our own moon.

I am becoming involved with life, losing my fear and letting go of people and things that interfere with my freedom and happiness.

APRIL 28

Although the world is full of suffering, it is full also of the overcoming of it.

Helen Keller

Human beings have an enormous capacity to endure hardships and heartbreak. If their spirits are not broken, people can emerge from what seem like impossible circumstances to not only overcome the difficulties, but be enriched by them. It is when our spirits are broken that we are defeated and embittered by misfortune.

Co-dependent people emerge from the chaos of childhood with different degrees of brokenness. Some do not make it. Many remain emotionally numb, but others plant their feet in the ground of recovery and grow.

I have the courage within me to go through the process of recovery.

APRIL 29

A good indignation brings out all one's powers.

Ralph Waldo Emerson

As children living in dysfunctional families our dignity and self-respect were trampled on year after year by unjust treatment. We had no way of knowing that this behavior was the result of illness, we had no choice but to assume it was our fault. At that time we were powerless to stand up on our own behalf.

We have every right to be indignant about what happened to us when we were young.

In recovery we learn to express our indignation in ways that help us to grow and to stand up for ourselves. We learn that although we are powerless to change the behavior of others, we have within us everything we need to become all that we want to be.

With the help of my Higher Power I am regaining my dignity and self-respect.

APRIL 30

Be what you are. This is the first step toward becoming better than you are.

Julius Charles Hare and Augustus William Hare

Who we are was misplaced in the rubble of childhood. Needing an identity, we were forced to recreate ourselves from imagination into what we thought a grownup was like. We then proclaimed these make-believe persons to be our authentic selves. Considering the difficulty of our task, we didn't do badly. The main flaw in our creation is that we are lopsided.

Healing is to shift around, even out the weight of ourselves by balancing and accepting our strengths and weaknesses. We can take off a few of our hats and forgive ourselves for imagined or real failures.

When we accept who we are, we can truly better our lives and ourselves.

I am learning to know and accept myself.

MAY 1

Give sorrow words . . .

Shakespeare

Unspoken grief manifests itself obliquely when it cannot find direct expression. It can find release in anger or chronic depression that saps the life force from us, or it can attack our bodies and make us physically sick. We cannot wish it away, will it away or give it away until we have discharged it as genuine sorrow.

Sorrow is our way of letting go of something or someone that was important to our lives. Joy and sorrow are linked, and when we don't process grief, our ability to experience joy is hampered. And without moments of joy, life seems hardly worth the effort.

I pray for the courage to grieve my losses.

MAY 2

Laughter is both an act of protest and an act of acceptance.

W. H. Auden

Think about it. What makes us laugh the most is the very thing that can make us the saddest. When we laugh, we are accepting and letting go at the same time. It is the Serenity Prayer uttered in mirth.

It's probably not by accident that if we laugh hard enough, tears stream from our eyes. It seems that by divine invention our funny bone is connected to our heart strings — a built-in safeguard to being overwhelmed by the tragedies of life.

As we deal with the issues of recovery, we should not overlook the importance of learning to laugh genuinely. It is as important to our well-being as learning to cry.

I am learning to use the God-given gift of laughter to help soften the pain in life.

MAY 3

Let us not look back in anger or forward in fear but around in awareness.

James Thurber

When we have done our emotional homework, the past will lose its power over us, and when we learn to let tomorrow happen in its own time, the only thing we will need to concern ourselves with is the here and now. To cease discharging energy in every direction, wasting it on the past or the future, is to give ourselves to the moment.

The only day that really matters is today. I will live it as fully as I know how.

MAY 4

I love you, warts and all.

Warts? Some of us have a lot of them — thank heavens! Warts make us interesting, approachable, likable. Our little imperfections let others know we are of this earth, not yet ready to don our heavenly halo.

Wartless people are suspect. How did they go through life and not catch them? What is tucked away in the folds of their gowns? Vulnerability, you say?

Co-dependents feel that if we're not perfect — if we have warts — then we're worthless, good-for-nothing failures. With that edict hanging over our heads, it's no wonder we try to cover up our warts.

But when we hide our warts, we also hide the best part of ourselves. The part that's forgiving, warm, spontaneous and raring to live life to its fullest.

I love me, warts and all.

MAY 5

And you begin to accept your defeats
With your head up and your eyes open
With the grace of woman, not the grief of a child . . .

Kara DiGiovanna

It is the throbbing of the unresolved grief of childhood that makes new hurt so painful and overwhelming for co-dependent people. The old pain, needing expression, attaches itself to little and big hurts in the here-and-now and intensifies the hurt. Anything that hints at abandonment — like a friend forgetting to call — is magnified out of proportion. And when major heartache occurs, our sense of abandonment reduces us to total despair and helplessness.

In recovery we clear our hearts of past grief, making room to absorb the disappointments and hurts that come our way as adults. We become enabled to accept losses and grow beyond them with serenity.

Each day I grow in wisdom and maturity and I am grateful.

MAY 6

Boy: A noise with some dirt on it.

Most co-dependents have difficulty having fun. We knew how once. We were born with the ability; playing is how we first learn about life. But in all the seriousness going on around us, our skills rusted from lack of use.

That playful child still exists in us. Perhaps he is a loudmouth, rambunctious boy whose first loves are dirt and worms and lizards, and the icing in Oreo cookies. Or maybe she is a soft-voiced, thoughtful girl whose favorite games are jacks and hopscotch, and Simon Says, and playing Go Fish with her daddy. Whatever the child within us is like, he or she still has a need and a right to play.

Learning to play is an important part of my recovery. I will find the Buried Treasure hidden inside of me.

MAY 7

What poison is to food, self-pity is to life.

Oliver C. Wilson

Self-pity eats away at our core. Without an antidote, all that is whole will be consumed and we will live our lives as bitter victims.

As children we were helpless in the face of a dreadful disease, but we managed to survive. This is to our credit but to let self-pity taint our hard-earned survival is another loss.

We are not helpless as adults. Angry, frightened, depressed, numbed, but not helpless. We have choices. We don't have to blame and resent others. When we stop nibbling from the "Poor Me" apple, we can heal and begin to taste the sweetness that life has to offer.

Self-pity is self-defeat. When I stop feeling sorry for myself, I can begin to love myself and others.

MAY 8

Sitting still and wishing
Made no person great.
The good Lord sends the fish
But you must dig the bait.

Many co-dependents have a tackle box of information about recovery. We go fishing for new knowledge at meetings, workshops and conferences. We get hooked on tapes and books, know all the buzz words and spout jargon with the best of them. But until we take action at an emotional level, we won't reel anything in but knowledge. And knowledge is not what we're fishing for, it's what we're fishing *with*. Recovery is what we want at the end of our line. Until we cast our hearts into the sea, recovery will always be the one that got away.

Knowledge is for my head; recovery is for my heart.

Forgiveness is a funny thing — it warms the heart and cools the sting.

Dr. William Arthur Ward

Forgiveness is an essential part of healing. The following passage is an analogy of what happens when we are able to forgive those who have hurt us:

> It is a bitter cold night and a man is stumbling down icy streets, searching for a place to get out of the storm that rages around him. Windows are dark, the streets empty of people. The wind bites at his face, fingers and ears. The lonely man rounds a corner and sees the fading glow of embers from a fire. Numb with cold, he stirs the ashes, adds gathered branches and waits. Flames leap to life, and he rubs his hands together over their warmth. Feeling returns to his numbed hands, his feet, his face. And slowly the precious warmth penetrates inside to melt the aching chill that wraps around his bones.

When I forgive my past, I will find the warmth of love and the light of serenity.

MAY 10

He who hesitates is sometimes saved.

James Thurber

Proceed With Caution. Yield. Stop. Highway signs are easy to read and clear in their message. Humans have no such signs. We proceed down the road of life by the seat of our pants!

Experience provides the road signs. Taking the wrong turn teaches us small and large lessons.

Caution gives us the time needed to think through a knotty problem or hold our tongues when we'd like to lash out at someone. It gives us the pause we need to "act" rather than "react" to situations or people.

I will think through my actions and decisions. This way I have a choice whether to carry them through or not.

If you insist on standing still, stand aside; others may be going somewhere.

In recovery we're on the move. We have things to do, places to go, people to meet and a life to put together. This is serious business and it would be terrific if parents, siblings, children and spouses would come along with us willingly. But . . .

When other people, important to our lives, build their walls higher as we try to reach them, we have no choice but to climb down, go around and get on with the business of healing. Perhaps they'll take note of the direction in which we're heading and follow someday. Perhaps not. Growth is a personal effort, if others insist on standing in a stagnant pond, we're not obliged to stand passively with them.

I have a right to grow and to heal. I need to let go of controlling others and being controlled by others in order to recover and find wholeness.

MAY 12

It ain't no disgrace for a man to fall, but to lie there and grunt is.

Josh Billings

If we could meet Josh Billings in person, he might continue his quote thus so:

> "Yep, we all make 'em. Mistakes. Falling off the horse is part of learnin' how to ride. But, pardner, don't stay down in the dust and get trampled. Get up and get back on the critter. That's the way we do it in recovery.
>
> "And while we're talking about mistakes, let's talk about learnin' from them. Sometimes they're the best teachers around. When we hit the ground hard, we remember it in our bones.
>
> "Nope. Nobody gets through life without falling on his face — or parts south and to the rear. It ain't how we fall, but how we get up that makes the difference."

If I don't learn something when I make mistakes, I've bitten the dust for nothing.

MAY 13

What more people need is the faith of the little old lady who declined a last-minute invitation to a garden party because she had already prayed for rain.

The little old lady mentioned above is unusual in her faith. Most of us would say yes to the invitation and take an umbrella . . . just in case our prayers were heard.

Faith props us up when life is falling apart around us. It whispers words of comfort in our ears, pats our backs in encouragement and winks when no one is looking, as if to assure us that things will be okay or if not, that something else will turn up.

Faith is not a learned thing, not a belief. It is an attitude, a trusting that allows the unseen forces of life to work their magic. Faith is what propels us from the dark and into the light of spirituality.

I will trust in the process of recovery and have faith that with the help of a Higher Power I can heal.

MAY 14

Those who are ashamed of the past and afraid of the future don't find the present so hot either.

How can we possibly enjoy today when we are red-faced about the skeletons from our past and white with fear about the ghosts imagined in our future? We're like lost children whistling in the dark, afraid to look back or move forward.

The good news for the lost child is that there is help. But that help can't come until we call out from the bottom of our hearts. We can read about recovery, dream about recovery, talk about recovery, become expert about recovery, but until we encounter those dreaded skeletons and ghosts at gut-level, we can't recover. We will continue whistling in the dark.

When we muster up the courage to face our demons, we will be free of the shame of the past and unafraid of the future.

I can find my way out of the dark and into the light of recovery.

MAY 15

Worry is like a rocking chair — it keeps you busy but it doesn't get you anywhere.

Worry wears us down just as sure as a rocking chair wears down the rug beneath it. Back and forth we go, fretting away, wringing our hands, occasionally getting up to pace. And what have we accomplished? We've probably made mountains out of a few molehills, imagined the worst scenario possible and etched an indelible frown across our forehead.

Worry is fear with short fingernails.

Concern differs from worry; it causes us to take action. Concern for our well-being is what brings us to recovery programs, which help us to stop chewing on our nails and start chewing on the issues we need to deal with.

Instead of worrying, I will say the Serenity Prayer.

MAY 16

You must lose a fly to catch a trout.

George Herbert

Change. It's not easy. It requires choice, decision, determination. When we choose in favor of one thing, we feel unfaithful to the other. We'd like simple solutions, like the *eeny, meeny, miny, moe* of childhood choices, but we can't have that luxury if we want to be healthy adults.

When we give up dependent behaviors and beliefs and acquire healthy ones, we may feel a sense of loss even though the old ways were harmful to our well-being. When we change and become responsible for ourselves, it's harder. And at times we may feel drawn to return to the familiarity of letting someone else's behavior run our lives.

I choose recovery. With faith, determination and the support of others, I can change my life.

MAY 17

Trust everybody but cut the cards.

Finley Peter Dunne

Don't trust. That's one of the cardinal rules in dysfunctional homes. And we learn it well. But when we come across someone we feel we can trust, we have a tendency to be too gullible. It's that all-or-nothing thinking at work here, and it's our inability to discern boundaries. Having little or no trust in our own thoughts or feelings, we allow others to serve as emotional mentors.

In recovery we become our own mentor and begin to make new rules about trusting. We establish boundaries that protect us from people who are emotional marauders and grow in our ability to have faith in those who prove trustworthy. Most helpful of all, we learn to trust our own instincts, intuitions and feelings.

I will trust my own feelings and I will trust others until they prove to be untrustworthy.

MAY 18

Every dewdrop and raindrop had a whole heaven within it.

Henry Wadsworth Longfellow

Before recovering many Adult Children find it hard to respond to the beauty of nature. We are so preoccupied with our internal conflict that we can't give our attention to externals, no matter how awesome.

Among the gifts of recovery is the ability to at last give ourselves over to the spectacles of the natural world. As we turn outward, we are freed to see into the intricate soul of God's earth. And we are humbled by the wonder of it all.

I will fill my heart with the beauty around me.

MAY 19

A habit cannot be tossed out the window, it must be coaxed down the stairs a step at a time.

Mark Twain

Sometimes it requires changing to break habits; and other times it requires breaking habits to change. Which comes first . . . ? In this case we'd better choose the one that works.

Some habits are more ingrained. They took up residence in us long ago. When we tell ourselves we are ugly or lazy, we are repeating what we heard as children. When the old tapes start spinning, we can shut them off, replace them with words that are kind and loving and forgiving.

Other habits will disappear a step at a time as we alter our attitudes. Where there was resentment, there will be forgiveness. Where there was self-pity, there will be gratitude. Where there was fear, there will be courage.

Habits are acquired. I can choose to keep them or change them.

MAY 20

And ye shall know the truth, and the truth shall make you free.

John. VIII. 32

To be free of those clanking chains of our past, it is necessary to pry loose those feelings that have been bound, gagged and hidden away in the dark chambers of our minds. These feelings are not those of a monster who will run amuck if allowed expression. These feelings are those of a muted child who longs to be heard.

Because this small being has been held captive so long, it will let its sadness and anger be known in an intense manner at first. But given air to breathe, room to flex its withered muscles, assurance that it will not be held captive again, it will fulfill a desire to be healthy, whole and loving.

I give permission to the child within me to express the sadness and anger of a lost childhood.

MAY 21

Loneliness expresses the pain of being alone and solitude expresses the glory of being alone.

Paul Tillich

When we are at peace, solitude lifts us above the level of normal existence. It is a time of gathering, of renewal. In its quiet, we can transcend earth-bound cares and enter a realm where the whole of life is illuminated.

This kind of solitude is more than just being alone, it is a state of being. Whether we're surrounded by towering trees or a tower of laundry to be sorted, it gives us the same gift: A journey inward to communicate with our soul.

When I find serenity, being alone will be filled with life.

MAY 22

We do not drown in the tears of healing. We wash away our sorrow.

There is a fairy tale called "The Princess Who Couldn't Cry." It is about a King who is distraught because his daughter could not cry. He summoned storytellers from all over the land to try to make her shed tears. But, alas, when they told sad stories to the Princess, she kicked off her slippers and laughed. The King all but gave up when he happened upon a lad who said he could make her cry. It was simple. He made the Princess peel an onion!

This story is not unlike those of us who have numbed ourselves about the trauma of our past. We are afraid to feel, so we stay in a state of suspended emotion. To get to the feelings that are at our core, we have to peel the layers away. And like the irritants in an onion, only these emotions will make us cry.

I am learning how to express my sadness with tears.

MAY 23

Wisdom comes by disillusionment.

George Santayana

Many people are under the illusion that life owes them something, or that others will provide endless love and undying devotion, or that they can find security and happiness in things outside of themselves. When reality sets in, life knocks them down and roughs them up. Then they must choose between staying in the illusion and becoming bitter and cynical, or to wise up and grow up.

As I recover, I will grow in wisdom and find inner peace.

MAY 24

The only time to worry over past mistakes is when they don't teach you anything.

For successful people mistakes are building blocks. They pick up the toppled blocks, figure out what went wrong and begin rebuilding. And if the blocks fall a second and third time, well . . . surely there's something to be learned. Quite often mistakes teach what *not* to do — an important lesson.

But for others, making mistakes is paramount to mortal sin! Adult Children often feel this way. Anything short of perfection will be punished by the fires of our own hell.

As we heal, we will be able to lighten up, loosen up and let up on ourselves. Mistakes become teachers, not torturers.

Today when I make a mistake, I will forgive myself. Mistakes give me the opportunity to learn and to grow.

MAY 25

It's not easy being me.

Co-dependent

Before recovery most of us feel like misfits, and lonely. What a relief to discover that we are not alone, that we number in the millions. Like frogs after a storm, we're everywhere!

When we're ensconced with our own kind, we discover that although we are not unique in matters of the heart, all of us have gifts to share that are one of a kind.

Recovery is the process that makes being who we are not only easy, but a reason to leap with joy!

I am uniquely me but I'm no different from others in my basic human needs.

MAY 26

Often the test of courage is not to die but to live.

Orestes

Courage is not of muscle or mind, it is of the heart, and matters of the heart are difficult for us to face. They expose our vulnerability. This risk is so great that many of us choose to entomb the essence of ourselves.

Recovery gives us another chance at life but requires a great deal of courage. We must be willing to open a Pandora's Box of emotion, throw out what is useless, what is tainted with bitterness, and expose what is whole and vulnerable to the healing pain of sorrow. When we have done this, we will have chosen the most difficult, but most rewarding way to live life.

I want to live life to its fullest. I have the courage to feel, to grow and to change.

Friendship is almost always the union of a part of one mind with a part of another; people are friends in spots.

George Santayana

This definition of friendship has class. Its message has a reality that many too-sweet sayings about friendships lack. True-blue . . . for ever and ever . . . no matter what . . . sentiments belittle the meaning of genuine friendship. Being and keeping a friend takes effort, it requires boundaries, intimacy, and it changes as we change. The value of a good friend can't be summed up in a cute slogan.

Co-dependents have difficulty with friendship because we clamp on too tight and expect too much when we do make a friend.

I will give my friends space to be fully who they are and will ask that they do the same for me.

MAY 28

Only the hand that erases can write the true thing.

Meister Eckhart

It's not possible or even desirable to clean completely the slate of our past. We can erase the harmful things until they are faint enough for us to write over with our own truth.

We can erase words and replace them with whatever adjectives describe who we really are. Over the words, *guilt* and *shame,* we can write, *NOT RESPONSIBLE!* And when we are able, we can draw a heart around the names of our family and write, *FORGIVEN.*

Recovery is the chance to rewrite the lopsided script of our past. And with our new-found skills we can write our future as bold and beautiful as we dare!

The truth of the past and the promise of the future are in my hands.

MAY 29

Recognizing what we have done in the past is a recognition of ourselves. By conducting a dialogue with our past, we are searching how to go forward.

Kiyoko Takeda

Making amends is not an orderly process, but the first person on the list, the one we have injured the most is ourselves.

For years we have neglected our emotional needs, berated ourselves unmercifully and abused our bodies by deprivation or over-indulgence. In essence, we locked our true selves in the closet and threw the key away. The frightened impersonator who took our place owes us one gigantic apology. When we've made amends to, and forgiven ourselves, we are ready to sincerely make them to others we feel we have harmed.

Before I can make genuine amends to others, I must make amends to myself.

MAY 30

Laughter is a tranquilizer with no side effects.
Arnold Glasow

As we heal we learn to laugh at ourselves with love. We begin to see all the wonderful oddities and contradictions in people — little faults that endear others to us. We see that striving to be perfect is going far beyond the call of duty, and we discover that life does not need to be a duty, that it can be enjoyed. Life can be fun.

We were given the gift of laughter to help us survive the tribulations of living. The healing effects of laughter can't be underestimated. A laugh a day may be exactly what's needed to keep the doctor away!

Laughter is healing. I want to learn to take myself less seriously.

MAY 31

Self-trust is the essence of heroism.

Ralph Waldo Emerson

Every day of our lives we are bombarded with an arsenal of decisions to make, large and small. These choices have to be arrived at by intellectual and emotional processes. If our choices prove to be wise, it's to our credit, and if they were mistakes, we take responsibility. To stand or fall on our own cognizance is an act of courage.

In recovery, as we begin to trust, it includes trusting ourselves. We slowly learn to have faith in our intuitions, feelings and thoughts. We stop letting every Tom, Dick and Harriet dictate our lives. We stop going outside ourselves for what is available within.

I am learning to trust my thoughts and emotions.

JUNE 1

The free man is he who does not fear to go to the end of his thought.

Leon Blum

The law says that we are innocent until proven guilty. Co-dependents are not law-abiding in this case. Instead, we come down on ourselves like a stern judge waiting to pronounce sentence on any unkind thought that dares to ask for mercy in our court. No matter how benign the offense, how slight the infraction, we bring the full weight of our law with a merciless sentence of endless self-recrimination.

This sense of guilt was brought from childhood. When we stop giving the past the power to stand as judge, we will find freedom.

I will be more merciful toward myself.

JUNE 2

The play left a taste of lukewarm parsnip juice.

Alexander Woolcott

Act One of our lives was spent in a play that at best could be compared with lukewarm parsnip juice — a bubbling cauldron might better describe living in an alcoholic home. Born into this confusing play, we don't learn effective ways to live, so we enter Act Two and repeat the same plot, getting into relationships and situations that leave the same distaste in our hearts.

At any time we choose we can change the plot. Recovery gives us the skills to rewrite the script for Act Three, in which we are co-stars, not codependents. One in which at the end of each scene, we are left with the taste of honey.

I am learning new methods of living. I am letting go of old behaviors and feelings that keep me trapped in the past.

JUNE 3

Bad temper is its own scourge. Few things are more bitter than to feel bitter. A man's venom poisons himself more than his victim.

A slug's defense is to taste so bad, so acrid, that nothing — not a bird, a frog or a lizard would dare eat one. When we hold on to bitterness, it is like stuffing our innards with a daily diet of slugs.

Slug eaters are not nice to be around. They are easy to spot from the sour expression on their faces, and their readiness to spew their bad tempers and resentments at anyone who crosses their path.

These bitter folks can continue chewing on their unsavory diet and be miserable, or they can change their emotional eating habits and try savoring forgiveness.

With the help of my Higher Power I let go of bitterness and taste the sweetness of life.

JUNE 4

Men can starve from a lack of self-realization as much as they can from a lack of bread.

Richard Wright

What didn't happen to many of us as children is as crippling as what did happen. Childhood is prime time for creativity, education, developing skills and exposure to the larger world. We grew up behind bleak narrow walls, caught up in family chaos with little focus on our psyche and talents.

To read *The Velveteen Rabbit* or *Winnie-the-Pooh* at age 30 is both joyful and sad. So many years lost not knowing the wonder of the classic books for children. We lost major portions of childhood and our grief is legitimate and healthy. Recovery is to acknowledge and feel our losses but to focus now on our talents and attributes. Fortunately, we have many. Our task is to learn to use them to become self-realized and fulfilled.

It is my time to become all that I can be!

JUNE 5

The wisest man is just a boy who grieves that he's grown up.

Vincenzo Cardarelli

Adult Children were banished from the Kingdom of Childhood too soon. But within us a loyal child waits to explore and discover the Kingdom of Living, and we are the vessel in which this birth will take place.

Because our time to BE is long overdue, we feel bone-deep gratitude and a sense of awe when joy bubbles from us like a shaken soda pop. Perhaps we see and feel the magic more than those who had the good fortune to experience childhood to its fullest.

There is a quote in the Bible that says in part: ". . . but when I became a man, I put away childish things." For us, it is time to become as a child, take out childish things and feel the wonder.

I am learning to let the child within feel the magic of *BEING.*

JUNE 6

A good garden may have some weeds.

Thomas Fuller, M.D.

With all there is to do in a day, it is impractical and improbable to do everything just so. Something's got to give, and if we work it right, it doesn't have to be our health or hard-earned serenity!

Our tendency toward perfectionism encourages a sense of failure, even though we complete tasks or projects admirably. "It wasn't good enough," we apologize.

Life is much nicer when we pick and choose what projects will get our best efforts and which ones aren't worth the bother. If gardening is a first love, and we delight in the toil and in seeing the most lush garden ever, by all means, we should give it our all, try for perfection. But if weeding is an unwelcome chore, pull a few and name the rest wild flowers.

I do not have to do things perfectly to be worthwhile. I am worthwhile just as I am.

JUNE 7

Is life so wretched? Isn't it rather your hands which are too small, your vision which is muddled? You are the one who must grow up.

Dag Hammarskjold

At best, growing up is hard to do. Adult Children enter the arena of adulthood impeded by an inability to adequately express ourselves, trust others and feel our emotions. Our shattered sense of self is at the mercy of the four winds and it is all we can do to hold on so we won't be blown away by life.

As we recover, we stand firmer on the ground, let go of our external supports, then explore and enlarge our inner and outer world. With clear vision we reach further than we ever dreamed we could.

It is up to me to let go of helplessness and despair and become responsible for myself.

JUNE 8

Our reverence is good for nothing if it does not begin with self-respect.

Oliver Wendell Holmes, Sr.

When we revere something or someone, it can be from deep love and respect or it can be from deep fear. Adult Children are riddled with fear, and much of who and what we revere stems from this fear.

We put people on pedestals who don't belong there and bow down and scrape to people we perceive to have power. But where are we in this company of greats? At the bottom, of course.

When we learn to respect ourselves, we lose our fear, stop giving others power over us, and begin to see people in a more realistic light. Then the reverence we feel for others will spring from genuine love and admiration for who they are.

Today I will revere myself for having the courage to change.

JUNE 9

Wounds cannot be cured without searching.

Francis Bacon

The culprits that cause emotional wounds are much the same the world over. Loss, neglect, abuse and rejection leave scars on the human heart, and the earlier these traumas happen in life, the deeper they are inflicted.

Recovery is to search for the wounds and buried feelings surrounding them and bring them into the open. We will feel pain, but it is healing pain. With self-nurturing, support from others and the help of a healing power greater than ourselves, our wounds will slowly mend. It is never too late to begin our search.

If I am willing, I can overcome the wounds of my past.

JUNE 10

Zest is the secret of beauty. There is no beauty that is attractive without zest.

Christian Dior

If we are *unrecovering* co-dependents, we will thumb through magazines and compare our appearance with the gorgeous and handsome models and declare ourselves utterly and hopelessly homely.

All or Nothing. The Best or the Worst. The Most or the Least. These are the mottos that keep us feeling ugly, stupid and worthless.

In recovery we discover that Great In Between into which most of us fall. We accept our physical attributes and make the most of them, and if we fall short in current standards of beauty, so be it. When we are happy with ourselves, involved with life, it shows. And there is nothing more captivating than someone who glows with enthusiasm.

The more I accept who I am, the more beautiful I become.

JUNE 11

The morning is wiser than the evening.

Russian proverb

Proper rest is critical to our physical, mental and emotional well-being. Most days will present enough challenges and tasks to bog us down by evening. And when we are tired, we often revert to habits and behaviors that are not in our best interest, so we give up and give in to negative thinking and actions.

A good night's rest is a gift to ourselves. Sleep, like fog, rolls over the landscape of our minds, softens the edges, shrouds the cares of the day with welcome oblivion. It is a time of renewal and repair. And as the morning sun burns off the fog, we awake refreshed, wiser and filled with resolve.

I will include proper rest on my list of "Things To Do Today."

JUNE 12

Every day cannot be a feast of lanterns.

Chinese proverb

As children we became accustomed to revved-up, super-charged days. As unpleasant as it was, we became addicted to excitement; it helped us to feel alive as we played out whatever role we took on to survive in our troubled family. We grew up not quite knowing what to do with the hours of an ordinary day. And not knowing how to act or interact with healthy people, many of us entered marriages with others of our own kind and recreated the chaos in which we knew how to function.

In recovery we begin to appreciate the ho-hum of everyday living. We learn that perhaps that which we once felt was boring is not. A good book, a stroll in the woods, raising guppies become pleasant activities.

As we seek excitement from within the glare we once sought is replaced with delight in the soft glow of paper lanterns.

Today I will seek quiet activity and companionship that calm and soothe my senses.

JUNE 13

I postpone death by living, by suffering, by error, by risking, by giving, by losing.

Anais Nin

How fully we have lived when the final curtain falls on our life is a matter of choice. Have we participated in the play? Or have we sat in the darkened theater and merely observed? If we have never had the courage to get up on stage without a script and emote without fear of consequences, then have we really ever known what being human is all about? It *is* a question of "To be or not to be . . ."

Being human is not an easy task for anyone, harder yet for those of us whose beginnings were shaky. But the rewards for exploring and sharing the depths of ourselves with others make the risks worthwhile.

I am learning to be fully alive, willing to risk and am losing my fear of life.

JUNE 14

It is with narrow-souled people as with narrow-necked bottles: The less they have in them, the more noise they make in pouring it out.

Alexander Pope

We all know the sound liquid makes as it gurgles through the narrow neck of a bottle, raising in pitch higher and higher as it empties out into another container. People with narrow minds and many opinions pour out their contents much the same way. With narrowed eyes, they spill out dogmas, their voices raising in fervor as they drench those around them with their hollow words. Oh, for the want of a cork!

Not wanting to hurt the feelings of others and fearing rejection, Adult Children are hesitant to walk away when being harangued by insensitive people. We need to learn that it's okay to stay out of harm's way. Why risk drowning our hard-earned serenity in their shallow pool?

I have a right to protect myself from unkind people with small minds.

JUNE 15

However broken down the spirit's shrine, the spirit is there all the same.

Nigerian proverb

We come to therapy and recovery programs broken and in need of repair. We hurt everywhere and nowhere. Weary from trying just to hold our heads above water, we give up the struggle — the denial — that only pulls us down deeper into our despair. It is the realization that we are drowning that causes us to cry out for help.

We are not aware that deep within us there is a quiet place flickering with light waiting for our return. When we folded our feelings away, we tried also to snuff out this light. We cursed it, said that it had failed us, that we had no use for it. We turned our backs and went our way alone.

As we recover and work our way through our darkness, we become conscious of this flickering and find the sanctuary within.

In recovery I will find my lost spirituality.

JUNE 16

True miracles are created by men when they use the courage and intelligence that God gave them.

Jean Anouilh

The unfolding of a co-dependent Adult Child is a remarkable phenomena to behold. Recovery is like a journey to Oz. Like Tin Man, Scarecrow and Cowardly Lion we discover that we have a heart, a brain and courage.

This transformation is indeed a miracle. What was stunted, blossoms; what was rigid, relaxes; what was bent, straightens; what was numbed, tingles with life.

The quote, "What you can become, you are already," sums up why we are able to make miracles happen. Our Creator instilled in us the desire to be whole and open to love. We need only take the spiritual journey inward to discover who we are.

My Higher Power gave me everything I need to be a miracle worker.

JUNE 17

I'm in search of myself. Have you seen me anywhere?

Once upon a time a wingless little bird hopped about sadly chirping, "Who am I? Who am I?" The other birds ignored him. When the days began to cool, the other birds flew South, and the little bird hopped after them. A few months later he looked up to see the others flying back so he turned around and hopped North. Season after season the little bird hopped back and forth but never arrived.

One day he saw a rose bud unfolding into a flower. "How did you do that?" he asked.

"I'm a rose, I'm supposed to unfold into a sweet-smelling bloom. Why are you *hopping* North?"

"I don't know. I don't know who I am. Do you?"

"Yes, you are a bird. You are supposed to sing, unfold your wings and fly."

"I'm a bird? I can fly? I can sing?"

"You only have to believe for it to come true."

With that the bird unfolded his wings and flew to the treetops, singing, "I am. I am."

At long last I am finding who I am.

JUNE 18

Men are not against you. They are merely for themselves.

Gene Fowler

When we are insecure within ourselves, it is easy to feel slighted by even the benign behavior of others. We take personally things that were not meant to offend and think that others are talking behind our backs. What we are doing is projecting on to them our own negative feelings about ourselves.

The truth is we don't take up that much time in the thoughts of productive people. They are busy with their lives, busy getting their own needs met.

As we recover we realize that the eyes of the world are not focused on us.

Today I will look after my own needs and allow others the space to do the same.

I have never seen a greater monster or miracle in the world than myself.

Montaigne

Each of us has the capacity to love and to hate. When we are at peace with ourselves, we have no cause to bare our fangs and hurt people. It is when we are full of self-hate and self-doubt that we lash out at others.

Recovery reaches into our core and repairs that part of us that is hurting and hating, and it enhances and enlarges what is lovable and loving. When we allow this healing to take place, we have enriched our lives and the people who share it with us.

I let go of hate and despair and replace them with love and hope.

JUNE 20

I'm glad I don't have to explain to a man from Mars why each day I set fire to dozens of little pieces of paper, and then put them into my mouth.

Mignon McLaughlin

When we stand back and look at addictions visually, they appear ridiculous. How would it look to a man from Mars to see us humans guzzle booze until we keel over or all of the other destructive things we do to medicate our pain? I would imagine this is why we haven't been invaded by Martians — they're afraid it might be contagious!

And in a sense, it is. Addictive and co-dependent behavior is everywhere. Co-dependency is glorified in popular song with lyrics proclaming, "I'm nothing without you." Television and magazines glamorize alcohol and cigarettes.

But we have a choice. We can continue on our "eat, drink and be merry-less" way or we can stop and face what ails us. When we give up harmful addictions, we can become addicted to the joy of life.

I want to feel my feelings and become addicted to life!

JUNE 21

It is the heart always that sees before the head can see.

Thomas Carlyle

Healing from the emotional wounds of our past is under the domain of the heart, the mind can only assist. It is possible to heal without knowledge, but impossible to heal without feeling.

Knowing what the problem is is helpful and comforting. It is a relief to learn that we are not different, and that the cause and effect of our dysfunction is predictable. It frees us to get down to the business of recovering.

With or without this information, when we have the courage to unwrap the bundle of despair within the depths of us, we will begin the journey that ends in a miracle.

I have the courage to open my heart to healing.

JUNE 22

Be a friend to thyself, and others will be so too.

Thomas Fuller, M.D.

We are drawn to people who treat themselves with respect and kindness. They are comfortable with who they are, and their ease helps us to relax.

As we learn to replace the childhood put-downs we received (and believed) with positive feelings about ourselves, we will become our own best friend. We will stop searching for flaws in the person we see in the mirror, stop harping at every little mistake we make and stop trying to bend over backwards for others while we neglect our own needs. And in our newfound esteem we know that the lonely, friendless days are gone forever.

Today I will respect my needs and treat myself with compassion.

JUNE 23

How poor are they who have no patience! What wound did ever heal but by degrees?

Shakespeare

Like physical wounds, emotional wounds heal imperceptibly from the inside out. A knitting together takes place, fiber by fiber until one day we all of a sudden have a healing. Patience and openness to change has allowed the miracle to occur.

Occasionally we are blessed with thunderbolt healings and we are grateful. These are gifts. But most healing comes a little at a time as we are willing and able to change and grow.

Recovery is a process that requires patience — lots of it — and respect for the small miracles that occur daily that lead toward wholeness.

Each day I have the opportunity to heal. I need only to persist and have patience.

JUNE 24

It is something — it can be everything — to have found a fellow bird with whom you can sit among the rafters while the drinking and boasting and reciting and fighting go on below.

Wallace Stegner

Finding ourselves, then finding healthy relationships is the goal of recovery. To find a loved one and share in a rich companionship is one of the most precious things we can experience in life.

When two healthy humans enter a relationship, they have the necessary ingredient it takes to get off to a good start — they feel complete unto themselves. Their desire for companionship is not based on a dependent need, but on mutual respect and love for the uniqueness of the other.

When I find who I am and hold myself in esteem, I will have what I need to enter loving relationships.

JUNE 25

A wounded deer . . . leaps highest.

Emily Dickinson

The following poem expresses the feelings of an Adult Child who is finding her way.

The Fawn

Newborn, I wobble
on spindly legs,
take my first step free
from the tangle of the past.
Alert, eager, I venture
toward the open meadow.
Guided by instinct, I know
I must keep distance
until I am stronger.
If you were to touch me now,
my legs might buckle.

I must learn to stand, to walk and to run. Then I will be ready to leap as high as I dare.

(Poem by Mitzi Chandler)

JUNE 26

Honey in one spoon
Medicine in the other
Reluctant child . . .
Determined mother.

Picture a child with scrunched face as he swallows a tablespoon filled with cod-liver oil. "Take this, it will make you healthy," he is assured. Does he believe it? Not on your life. He is doing what he has to do.

Healing is like that. We have to take it on faith that it will make us feel better. Others have told us that it will. So we take a big gulp and let the medicine go down . . .

And slowly we learn that it does make us better and better. In fact, we learn we never knew how bad we felt until we learn what it feels like to be well. And we are very grateful we had the courage to open our hearts to taste the sweetness of healing.

As I heal, each day will become sweeter and sweeter.

JUNE 27

Tolerance often gets the credit that belongs to fear of rejection.

Adult Children grow up built to withstand earthquakes, tornadoes, floods and fire. But we are not built to withstand even the slightest rejection — imagined or real. It is our Kryptonite. To protect ourselves, we contort ourselves to accommodate people and situations and call it tolerance.

As we recover we learn the difference between a backbone and a rubber spine. We begin to stand tall for what we believe in and what we are willing to put up with. We become able to confront rejection without becoming incapacitated. And we gain genuine tolerance for others, allowing them to be who they are.

I am learning to stop tolerating behavior and situations that are harmful to my well-being.

JUNE 28

The secret thoughts of a man run over all things, holy, profane, clean, obscene, grave and light, without shame or blame.

Thomas Hobbes

The above statement is not true for Adult Children. Yes, we have the myriad thoughts that run through the human mind, but we feel great shame about thoughts we consider to be bad. And, of course, we blame ourselves, accuse ourselves of being terrible people for harboring such thoughts.

But the truth is that until we give it power, a thought is but a flimsy thing that floats by our mind's eye. It is of no consequence unless we dwell on it or act on it.

In recovery when one of those "awful" thoughts pop into our head, instead of doing penance for our sin, we can merely let the little devil go by and get on with living and loving.

I am a human with free will. I have the capacity to pick and choose what thoughts and feelings to act on and which to let go.

JUNE 29

The ability to simplify means to eliminate the unnecessary so that the necessary can speak.

Hans Hofmann

Recovery is a process of simplification. We have spent most of our lives disconnecting and splicing our emotional wires until our inner workings are frayed, tangled and short-circuited. The simple math of our emotions becomes as difficult to decipher as calculus.

Although we have our wires crossed, all the parts we need to get our feelings humming with healthy responses are intact. We can make life even easier by reaching out and reconnecting with our Higher Power.

I am learning to be in touch with and respond to my feelings.

JUNE 30

Would that life were like the shadow cast by a wall or a tree, but it is like the shadow of a bird in flight.

The Talmud

Like clouds in transition, we move across the expanse of our lives until we are no more. We are part of a continuum, our stay on this earth but a brief passage.

Most of us fear death. But knowing that time is precious and must not be squandered can help us to live richer lives. If our days and nights were endless, they would have little value, and we would greet sunrise with indifference, the moon would hold no magic and stars would not be for wishing.

The length of our lives is up to the gods, but the depth and breadth of life is under the domain of the human heart.

I will live as fully as I can today.

JULY 1

A misty morning does not signify a cloudy day.

Ancient proverb

Those who live by the sea know from experience that the fog shrouding the shores will burn off as the summer sun rises higher in the sky. They bide their time, knowing that more than likely the sky will be clear and blue in a few hours. Those not familiar with this phenomenon may well pack their blankets and picnic baskets and go home, believing the whole day will remain gloomy and overcast.

Seeing beyond the next moment, looking on the bright side of things, believing that circumstances can change given time and effort, all enhance our ability to cope with the inevitable times when our lives are banked in clouds.

If I expect that things will improve, they will.

JULY 2

Every vice is only an exaggeration of a necessary and virtuous function.

Ralph Waldo Emerson

Once upon a time addictions were called vices, wrong-doings, the work of the devil. Now we know them to have their basis in psychological and physiological dependencies. And with the devil out of the picture, we have been able to get to the root of these behaviors that cause so much pain.

Those of us with dysfunctions and addictions have developed faulty means of meeting our needs. We use a bucket with a gaping hole in the bottom in an attempt to fill them.

In recovery we learn that our bucket *has* a hole, and we begin the process of repairing it. When we do this, we are on our way to filling ourselves with the essentials for a happy, healthy life.

I am learning to fulfill my needs in healthy ways.

JULY 3

The weak can be terrible because they try furiously to appear strong.

Rabindranath Tagore

The word *weak* has many meanings. For our purpose, let's define it as *lacking power.* When people are emotionally isolated and embittered, they are full of fear. And fear looks furious when its hackles are raised.

Many of us grew up in homes where in order to survive, we had to put up our guard, learn to swing back — physically and emotionally. We didn't start out to be bullies, we were afraid and needed to protect ourselves.

When we look behind our fear, we will see hurt and a sense of helplessness. And when we look further yet, we will discover a lonely human who wants to love and be loved. Then we need to look no further, for we will have found ourselves.

Today I will not be too quick to ruffle my feathers. I can respond in nonthreatening ways when I am angry or afraid.

JULY 4

Personal liberty is the paramount essential to human dignity and human happiness.

We all want to be free. Democracy provides us with liberty unparalleled in the world but freedom from the tyranny of our past is up to us.

Humans are born small and helpless, dependent upon our caretakers until we develop skills to become self-sufficient. In alcoholic homes, living skills are not imparted adequately and we are forced to bend in distorted ways to survive. We grow to adulthood in body, but our emotional selves remain unskilled and tangled in the past.

Recovery gives us the opportunity to pull loose from the past, to declare our independence and become all that we can be.

Today I celebrate my freedom.

JULY 5

Suffering isn't ennobling, recovery is.

Christiaan N. Barnard

Ennobling has to do with dignity. And there is no dignity in relentless pain that erodes away the very essence of who we are. Suffering without love to nurture us can embitter humans, turning us into misshapen beings, empty and hardened.

What is ennobling is that the human spirit can be brought back to life. If but a small spark remains, it can be rekindled by love. And with this healing, our dignity will be restored.

I am regaining my sense of dignity.

JULY 6

A road that does not lead to other roads always has to be retraced, unless the traveler chooses to rust at the end of it.

Tehyi Hsieh

A journey can take many shapes. It can be a circle leading nowhere, a confusing maze, a boxed-in square, a straight line leading to a dead end or it can be an upward spiral. We can change the shape of our journey at any time along the way.

The road to recovery is an upward spiral. It is open-ended and will stretch as far as we choose to travel. There are places to rest, and view points to look back or forward. The road weaves in and out of sunshine and shadows as it expands upward.

The road to recovery begins when we take our first step over the border of denial.

I am on a road that leads to health, happiness and serenity.

JULY 7

Men tire themselves in pursuit of rest.

Laurence Sterne

Most co-dependents are intense humans, doing whatever it is we're doing with a vengeance. Jaws clamped, we jackhammer our way through life.

Our attempts at relaxation are disquieting rather than restful. We are so intent on organizing, on controlling, on doing it perfectly that we often end up more frazzled than we were before.

We need to learn to relax our jaws, our grip, our muscles, our guard and our expectations.

There are ways we can soothe the jouncing within us. Meditations and affirmations help redirect our thinking, warm baths and exercise will draw dis-ease from our body, companionship with understanding friends can quiet our hearts and the Serenity Prayer will provide comfort for our souls.

Today I will work "easy" at trying to relax.

JULY 8

The trouble with some people is that they want to get to the Promised Land without going through the wilderness.

Most of us are in a hurry to recover and want the easiest route to get there. That's understandable. We've spent our lives struggling to survive. We're weary and time is wasting. So we read and read and read all the good news about recovery. Informed, we tap one foot then the other, and wait for healing to take place. When nothing happens, we don't understand why.

Nothing happens because we are expecting to find the treasure without going on the hunt. Knowledge provides direction and instructs us as to what to expect along the way. But it is our hearts that must make the long journey.

I am *feeling* my way out of the wilderness.

JULY 9

Who is there that can make muddy water clear? But if allowed to remain still, it will become clear itself . . .

Lao Tzu

The key to self-discovery, the way to peace and spirituality, can be gleaned by breaking down the following passage from the Bible:

"Be still and know that I am God."
Be still and know that I am.
Be still and know.
Be still.
Be.

Today I will listen to the quiet of myself.

JULY 10

Keep doing what you're doing and you'll keep getting what you're getting.

Johnny Harris

Like a boomerang, whatever we throw out has a way of turning around and coming back to us. If we hurl negative attitudes, they will return and bonk us in the head. If we toss out positives, they will return and land gently at our feet.

When things are going well for us, we are obviously doing something right. But we often forget or don't realize that our actions cause equal and corresponding reactions.

In recovery we start looking. Looking at our actions and reactions to people and situations, at how and why we get in our own way, and at what it is that causes us to behave in self-defeating ways. We slowly turn it around, replacing negatives with positives.

I replace old behaviors and attitudes with healthy ones.

JULY 11

Don't be afraid to say you are sorry. Nobody got indigestion yet from eating his words.

Co-dependents are apology prone. We kowtow our way through a day, apologizing to strangers, friends and foes for our benign offenses. This is not the kind of apology we are addressing here. We are talking about our inability to say, "I'm sorry," to significant others in our lives when we have been at fault.

We find it difficult to apologize because of our fear of giving up control and we feel we are in competition and to apologize is admitting defeat.

When we break our desperate need for control, those fence-mending words, "I'm sorry," will open the way for genuine communication.

I am learning to apologize when I am wrong and stand my ground when I am right.

JULY 12

How unhappy is he who cannot forgive himself.

Publilius Syrus

Co-dependents are riddled with guilt, most of it carried over from that which was heaped on us as children. And in our adult life that guilt attaches itself to everything we do. Our egos are fragile and our conscience and sense of responsibility overdeveloped.

To feel regret when we have harmed someone is natural. The only thing that can be done is to make amends, learn from it and forgive ourselves. From there we can grow and become wiser and more compassionate.

As we heal and let go of the guilt that doesn't belong to us, we can forgive ourselves, leaving us free to grow and put our best efforts into what *is* and what *will be.*

I am letting go of guilt that is not mine to own, and accepting responsibility and making amends for behaviors that have hurt others.

JULY 13

I sought my soul but my soul I could not see.
I sought my God but my God eluded me.
I sought my brother — and I found all three.

Anonymous

The first thing that many of us do when we "get religion" is to reach up rather than reach out. With arms stretched high, we grab hold of a lofty cloud only to have it vanish. Disillusioned, we tumble to earth wondering where we went wrong.

What went wrong is that we overlooked humanity. Before beginning our spiritual search, we clutched our arms across our chests, keeping others out and ourselves hidden.

Spirituality begins with love and openness of self. As love flows between human hearts and they reach out to each other, in this overflowing they discover the wonder that is God.

Today I will reach out to give and to receive.

JULY 14

Hell, Madam, is to love no longer.

Georges Bernanos

We enter this world with love tucked into our seams. If the seams split from neglect or misuse, love slowly seeps out and profound sadness enters. Without repair this sadness deadens our responses or turns to hate. And when our core smolders with hate, life burns and this burning consumes us.

Our natural state is love. And love is innocent, tenacious with the power to overcome hate. To rid ourselves of hate and recapture love's essence, we must seek the loving hands of a Higher Power. With this help we can douse the burning and be restored to our natural selves. This is the miracle of a second birth.

I was born to love and be loved. I can find my way back to this natural state.

JULY 15

Let my heart be wise. It is the gods' best gift.

Euripides

There is a quiet voice within us that we can't hear over the din of denial. Our mind clamors in its effort to keep hidden what it doesn't want to acknowledge. But there are moments when this voice from deep within our heart cries out in despair. We hear, begin to feel and the clamoring increases in an attempt to block the pain. Some of us spend our lives buried beneath this blare of discord.

Recovery begins when we call a halt to the tumult and face our denial, then awash in healing pain, we give ourselves to the wisdom of the heart.

I am on a journey that will lead me from the shadows into the sun.

JULY 16

A kindness goes a long way lots o' times when it ought t' stay at home.

Kim Hubbard

For the most part, co-dependents are a kindly lot. In fact, we are some of the most generous and compassionate humans around. That is, to everyone except ourselves!

The Golden Rule for co-dependents should be:

Do unto yourself as you would do unto others.

Today I will be as kind, considerate, respectful and forgiving to myself as I am to others.

JULY 17

The kids are gone and the dog just died.

Adult Child

"We stayed together for the children." "It's against my religion to divorce." "I just can't hurt him." "I'm afraid to be on my own."

For whatever reason, many of us swept the problems plaguing our marriages under the rug. Over the years lumps formed under the shag and we tripped over them daily without comment, pretending they were part of the decor.

Then something happens. A small thing, a large thing, and we are forced to look at what's hiding under the carpet.

As we heal we become better equipped to throw back the rug and begin sweeping out the problems. This is difficult, and it will take time for the dust to settle, but it can lead to a new beginning in our relationship.

I will look at what is healthy and what is in need of repair in my marriage.

JULY 18

There are two kinds of people: those who say to God, "Thy will be done," and those to whom God says, "All right, then, have it your way."

C. S. Lewis

Most of us retract what we say we are going to do in the Third Step. We turn our will over then when the heat is on, we grab it back and do it our way. If we do this often enough, and for long periods of time, the Higher Power sighs like an exasperated parent, determines we are not ready for His help, and lets us bungle our way until we hurt enough to try it again, His way.

When we let go of our Higher Power, we latch on to those around us in a tottering dance of dependency. And when we drop from exhaustion from trying to do it our way, we can either stay down or retrace our steps and do it His way. The choice is ours.

•

Today I will let my Higher Power work miracles.

JULY 19

Inches make champions.

Vince Lombardi

We would do well to follow the example of an inchworm as it loops its body slowly and persistently toward the succulent leaves at the end of a branch. It nourishes itself then builds a cocoon in which it patiently waits to evolve into what it will become — a beautiful creature with wings. Its inching days over, it flies free.

Recovery is a slow process so we need persistence to see it through. It takes a belief that we are fulfilling our destiny as we inch our way across the branch of discovery, and as we wait out the imperceptible process of change. And when we have evolved enough to leave our cocoons, it takes courage to unfold our delicate wings and fly.

I will take it an inch at a time.

JULY 20

Love is Nature's second sun.

George Chapman

The earth revolves around the sun absorbing the light and warmth that is necessary for human existence, while the human heart absorbs the light and warmth of love in order to thrive. Without love, life is as bleak and desolate as a planet without sun.

Recovery is a dawning, an awakening to the possibility of love. And in our new day we can begin to discharge the angry currents that churn within and let sadness fall gently from our hearts. When we do this, we will feel the warmth and light that is love, and with the return of the sun we will discover the miracle of rainbows.

I welcome this new day filled with the possibility of love.

JULY 21

Resolve to be thyself; and know that who finds himself, loses his misery.

Matthew Arnold

In our fear of abandonment and need for approval at all cost, we sell ourselves down the river. We behave like parrots repeating what others say, like monkeys mimicking what others do, and we change like chameleons to whatever color it is we need to be to gain acceptance. All the while our true selves cower beneath layers of denial in frightened despair.

When we claw our way up from the frozen ground and shake off the clumps of our past, we are free to be the unique creatures we were intended to be, not imitations or appendages of others. And when we begin to speak our own minds, live our own lives and show our true colors, we will hold our heads high and feel proud and grateful to be who we are.

In expressing my true self, I am discovering my true worth.

JULY 22

Lives of great men all remind us
We can make our lives sublime
And, departing, leave behind us
Footprints on the sands of time.

Henry Wadsworth Longfellow

At ebb tide we may see footprints imprinted in the smooth sand. The patterns vary: a focused circle, a flowing weave, oblique impressions that disappear in the surf and prints that seem to lead nowhere. So it is with our lives.

We can walk gently on this earth and leave behind wisdom and love, or we can walk heavily and leave behind ignorance and hate. We can also choose to walk in apathy and leave nothing at all. And at anytime on our journey we can change the impressions we make.

Recovery is the incoming tide that washes the shore of old impressions, leaving an untrodden expanse for us to explore.

I want to leave behind footprints of love.

JULY 23

God offers to every mind its choice between truth and repose. Take which you please — you can never have both.

Ralph Waldo Emerson

Denial is self-deception plain and simple. But the cause of our denial is as complex to us as the troubled homes we grew up in. By the time we're old enough to reason, our emotions aren't reasonable anymore; they are constricted and confused. We try to make order out of chaos by use of denial and control.

Other Adult Children who are further down the road to recovery can be of genuine help when we are stuck in denying our denial. They were once in the same rut and they know what we need to hear to help us out. We won't always like what they have to say, but in our hearts we know they are right.

With the help of a Higher Power and others who care, I am overcoming denial.

JULY 24

None preaches better than the ant. And she says nothing.

Benjamin Franklin

It is impressive to sit beside an ant hill and watch legions of tiny ants scurry in purposeful work. By their example we observe what persistence and working together can accomplish. (Only one person has ever reported that as they sat quietly watching, one of the little critters stopped what he was doing, stood on his hind legs, looked up and delivered a sermon on the importance of hard work! But then . . . that story ran in a tabloid next to a column about an Adult Child who had no denial.)

What we do speaks louder than what we say. What we say can be wrong. The best way we can genuinely help others, while at the same time help ourselves, is to repair our own heart and let it speak for itself. Our example gives others the opportunity to see for themselves what recovery can accomplish.

I want to be a teacher, not a preacher.

JULY 25

There is nothing either good or bad, but thinking makes it so.

William Shakespeare

The *tone* of a book is the attitude from which the author is writing. Each page will be consistent with the tone the author chose. So it is with our attitudes and they will determine the tone of our life.

If our interior dialogue is filled with four-letter feelings, it will show up in our behavior. We will approach people and situations with hostility, resentment and a get-even attitude. The book of our life may well be called, *It's A Dog-Eat-Dog World,* by Self Pity.

To change the tone of our life we need to understand why we have a negative point of view, and what we can do to correct it. We will then break our book down into 12 chapters, following the tone of the Steps to change our story to one in which the main character overcomes all odds and ends up a winner.

I cannot change the past, but I can change my attitude towards it.

JULY 26

It ain't over 'til it's over.

Yogi Berra

All Adult Children have a story to tell. Many tell of neglect and abuse so severe that it would seem they could not have survived. But survive we do and it ain't over yet. We want better than survival, we want wholeness of body, mind and spirit.

Upon hearing our stories, those from healthy homes shake their heads in disbelief, "How could you possibly live through what you did? How can you forgive what happened?"

Out of necessity, we were blessed with an extra measure of compassion and sensitivity. When we have done our grieving, expressed our rage and faced our fears, we can tap into that extra measure of humanity to understand and forgive those who hurt us. We can go beyond and become even more than we might have been.

I am grateful for not only my survival, but for the many blessings that recovery is unfolding for me.

JULY 27

Recovery is . . . enjoying life more and enduring it less.

Peggy Katherine Joseph

Before we reap the blessing of recovery, life is *H-A-R-D.* Weary of enduring and tired of the struggle, we seek help only to discover that recovery is harder than enduring. No fair! Who needs this? But something deep within us knows that there is no turning back, that although we are embarking on a turbulent journey, it has a silver lining.

In time the bumps level out and the traveling gets easier. We begin exploring the larger world, seeing its beauty, feeling its excitement, hearing it beckon. We respond with open arms, easy smiles and a grateful heart for we have found the silver lining.

Hallelujah!

JULY 28

You love me so much, you want to put me in your pocket. And I should die there smothered.

D. H. Lawrence

Co-dependents are addicted to the possibilities of people. We are attracted to lost souls who we can save. We need them to help fill the void in us.

Need is the issue here. *Our* need, not that of those we rescue. We believe that we are giving, but what we are really doing is taking. We are taking away their opportunity to make mistakes and learn from them. We are taking away their freedom to be who they are, for better or worse.

When we let go of our need to control, we can stop clutching, and start touching the lives of others by backing off and giving them room to breathe. This is what healthy caretaking is about.

Today is for self-care and self-repair.

JULY 29

May you live all the days of your life.

Jonathan Swift

Each day is an adventure and offers the opportunity for discovery. Why not take a walk on the wild side? Find a winding path through the woods and give yourself to the forest. Hear the trees whisper your name, and let the silence enfold you.

Discover the excitement of close encounters — venture beyond chitchat with others. Learn what their dreams are, what makes them laugh and cry. Tell them about your hopes and fears, how you feel about living and dying.

Love is the most daring adventure of all. Be generous in giving it, grateful in receiving it and unafraid in finding it around every corner.

This day is mine to savor.

JULY 30

This is one of those cases in which the imagination is baffled by the facts.

Winston Churchill

Expectations set us up for disappointment. In our minds we plan ahead for what might occur at a family get-together, what we will say "spontaneously" at the next session with our therapists, how someone should respond to a gift we've given or a favor we've done for them or how we will act at the next P.T.A. meeting. When things don't go as we imagined, we feel let down, cheated, mad at the world — and ourselves.

When we no longer expect people, places and things to comply with our emotional itinerary, we won't be setting ourselves up to be knocked down. Instead, we can relax, let happen what will happen and be grateful for unexpected pleasures.

Today I will wipe my slate clear of expectations and make room for surprises.

JULY 31

I have a ME!

Adult Child

When we break through the bedrock of denial and despair, it is like finding gold. We discover within our veins everything we need for richness of life. How joyful we feel! For the first time, we want nothing nor need nothing from others to feel complete. We know we were created by holy hands. We feel worthy, and our gratitude knows no bounds.

It is arduous work to search through the dark for our identities, but when we hold our newfound selves to the light, we know that it was well worth the digging.

I am finding me — a precious human being.

AUGUST 1

The imagination of a boy is healthy, and the mature imagination of a man is healthy; but there is a space of life between in which the soul is in a ferment, the character undecided, the way of life uncertain, the ambition thick-sighted.

John Keats

The span between the wonder of childhood and the wisdom of maturity is a long one. It is like the ocean between two shores, sometimes calm and rolling, sure of its destiny; other times swirling in turbulence unable to find its way. And like the ocean we are pulled to different shores. To remain transfixed in wonder is to give ourselves over to the care of others, and to take on the cloak of wisdom is to lose easy answers to life.

As I mature in wisdom I do not have to give up my sense of wonder.

AUGUST 2

Pepper calls attention to itself. That is its business. Salt, on the other hand (unless it is overdone), calls attention to what it salts.

Kenneth L. Wilson

Being humble doesn't mean that we can't acknowledge our virtues and talents, only that we be grateful for them, that we not strut them in boastful pride. And being humble allows us to graciously recognize and call attention to the virtues and talents of others.

To be humble is to recognize our shortcomings without succumbing to feelings of shame or worthlessness because we have flaws, and to be proud of what is well and good about us.

Humility is recognizing what is right in me, and what is wrong. Knowing these things about myself, I will not feel false pride nor will I feel ashamed of my imperfections.

AUGUST 3

A hypocrite is a fellow who isn't himself on Sundays.

Boswell Jones, a pious man, goes to church every Sunday, tithes and serves on the Newcomers Committee. On Sunday evening, Boswell Jones takes off his Sunday best and changes into his "real" clothes. The nicest thing that can be said of Boswell Jones from Monday through Saturday is that he is a cad and a womanizer. We could probably forgive him his faults if he weren't so dang pious and sneaky about them.

We cannot be perfect, but we can be what we seem. When we don't play games with ourselves, it won't be necessary to pretend to others to be something that we are not.

I will let my behavior say to others, "What you see is what you get."

AUGUST 4

Some days the dragon wins.

First it was the car, hopefully a minor problem. No such luck, it's the crankshaft. A mechanic pal said he could fix it, but it will take some time, a week or two. And where will she get the money to pay for it? Then the water main to the house burst — three days with no water. A heat wave, a cracked tooth, a nasty letter from a sister still in denial. Could anything else go wrong? Then Tuska dies. With his wagging tail and knowing eyes, he was more than woman's best friend, he was her family comfort.

We all have them — those times when problems pile up so high we can't see over them, and we can't unclench our teeth long enough to utter the Serenity Prayer. We need to reach out for moral support; eat light meals, but *do* eat; try to get enough rest but not sleep the problems away, they need our attention; and don't borrow trouble, this is not the time to take on anything else.

My friends and my Higher Power will see me through hard times.

AUGUST 5

Men go forth to wonder at the height of mountains, the huge waves of the sea, the broad flow of the ocean, the course of the stars — and forget to wonder at themselves.

Saint Augustine

Human beings are a blessing or a curse, depending on whose spell we're under. If we were to judge ourselves by what we see and hear daily in print and on television, it appears that we are a pretty sorry lot, out to destroy ourselves and our environment.

But people of goodwill abound in our world. We must not forget the wonder of ourselves, for with it we can help create a better earth, a better place in which all living things have a chance to come to fruition.

I am a child of the universe. I can make a difference in the world.

AUGUST 6

You Can't Go Home Again.

Thomas Wolfe

Until we begin to recover, we don't even *leave* home emotionally. Instead we continue in the same roles we took on as children to cope with the turmoil in our childhood homes. We discover that what worked then doesn't work now. Our attempts are like trying to mix oil and water. We can't. One outweighs the other no matter how furiously we stir.

We make our move by turning around and facing our pain squarely, then letting go of the apron strings that keep us tied to the past. Having done this, we can at last come home to ourselves.

I am building a new way of living for myself.

AUGUST 7

Gratitude is the heart's memory.

French proverb

As we heal we can at times be overwhelmed with gratitude. So grateful are we for our newfound life that we could shout it from tall buildings or dance in the rain like Gene Kelly did, singing out our joyous feelings. But most of us manage to contain these outbursts and instead share our gratitude with recovering friends.

It is the memory of how we were before recovery that makes our gratitude so profound. We were drowning and didn't know how to cry for help. And then something — a miracle, a rope, we don't know — came our way and we were pulled out of the depths and we struggled to shore.

Now, when our hearts remember the pain, they want to beat wildly with gratitude for the gifts of recovery.

I am grateful that each day, in every way, I am getting better and better.

AUGUST 8

One always begins to forgive a place as soon as it's left behind.

Charles Dickens

Co-dependents back into adulthood tugging the burdens of childhood with us. We don't know where to leave our bundle, so we take it with us everywhere until we can't go on any longer dragging the weight of it.

Recovery is the process of leaving this bundle behind. We cannot make peace with our past until we stop allowing its contents to spill out into the present.

When we break through denial it is as though we are letting go of the bundle for the first time. We will leave it behind and begin to walk with lighter steps, our hands free to swing by our sides, our hearts free to forgive those who hurt us.

I will be free of the past when I can forgive.

AUGUST 9

The resolve is always the same: never to be "thingafied."

Richard Foster

We live in a society that covets not only what the Joneses have, but what the Rockefellers and the Astors have. And with our gold-plated charge cards we may not keep up with the elite, but we certainly come in an impressive second — that is, until the monthly statements arrive in a wheelbarrow.

Part of our love affair with things is that it helps fill the emptiness. The world out there is sterile and lonely. We are the number on a charge card, the signature on a check.

"Things" are not our goal, we are on a spiritual quest. In our groups we discover the blessings of genuine friendships, and there isn't a "thing" in this world that we value more.

My goal is recovery.

AUGUST 10

For everything there is a season, and a time for every purpose under heaven . . .

Ecclesiastes

Spring came and went and many of us did not bloom. Instead we were struggling to untangle ourselves from the roots of our childhood.

Consider the chrysanthemum, the dahlia, perennials that blossom late in the season. Hardy, patient, they come into their own, not behind schedule, but in their season.

Late bloomers, we needn't bemoan what we might have been. Revere instead what we are. A miracle. A hardy survivor whose courage and tenacity, despite all, flourished. It is our season to unfold and reach for the sky.

Today I will hold my head high and revel in who I am.

AUGUST 11

If you are seeking creative ideas, go out walking. Angels whisper to a man when he goes for a walk.

Raymond Inmon

Many people believe creativity to be a mere amusement, something children and weird artists do, and most certainly a waste of time. What these unenlightened souls don't realize is that Heaven itself oversees creativity. It is our link with what is spiritual.

It is a noisy world. It hammers and buzzes and screeches and crashes and vibrates in our ears until we lose touch with the quiet within us. We need to step back from the chaotic kaleidoscope of sound and motion to reattach with our creative thoughts. A long walk, listening to music, quiet meditation, reading the inspired words of others, are all ways in which we can again hear the holy whispering. It is in these special moments that we transcend our limits and soar with the Angels.

Today I will get in touch with my creative thoughts.

AUGUST 12

Self-love, my liege, is not so vile a sin as self-neglecting.

William Shakespeare

Taking pride in how we look is a foreign concept to many of us. We neglect our appearance because we feel unattractive, and a "what's-the-use" attitude allows us to let ourselves go. We select drab clothing so we will not be noticed, attending to only the bare essentials of grooming.

As we recover we will begin to feel good about who we are and want our appearance to reflect our new feelings. We stop feeling guilty about spending a few bucks on ourselves. Best of all we look in the mirror approvingly at our new bright-eyed friend.

Today I will take some time for grooming. I am learning to like myself.

AUGUST 13

I feel like a "Godlette."

Adult Child

The reawakening of our spirituality is the greatest gift of recovery. This awareness that we are children of the universe, molded by the hands that created earth and the never-ending sky, gives us a sense of wonder and anticipation we've never experienced before. Gratefully we want to show our deep respect by taking on the qualities of love — the essence of God.

The Adult Child who proclaimed that she felt like a Godlette is well aware that she will never be able to love perfectly, forgive perfectly and understand perfectly, but she is willing to live her imperfect best. This is all that is asked of us by our Higher Power.

I gratefully accept my spiritual awakening.

AUGUST 14

Every human being is a problem in search of a solution.

Ashley Montagu

At best life is hard. Even the most fortunate have daily problems to overcome. We all live with the dangers and diseases that beset our world, and death waits in the shadows for each of us. This is the great common bond between humans and it helps to know that we are not alone.

Generations of people who have faced life boldly, overcoming great difficulties, pass down the message that life is precious and worth the effort. Their faith in life gives us courage to sieve through the difficulties and find the nuggets that line the river of life.

I welcome each day as an opportunity to discover the value of life. I pray that I will be open to giving and receiving love. I pray for a closer relationship with my God.

AUGUST 15

Adversity introduces a man to himself.

When we make the statement, "I'd go through that again if I had to," we are saying that although what we experienced was painful or difficult, what we gained from it was well worth the effort.

It would be untrue to say that all people are made stronger by hardship. Some are not. They are taken to the brink and beyond by too much adversity. For most of us, our attitude about misfortune can determine how we come out on the other end of tribulation.

When we unleash the natural healing powers within us to do their work, we will not only overcome the trauma of the past, we will build on it and become stronger in compassion and understanding than we might have been.

My loss can be my gain.

AUGUST 16

Honesty without compassion and understanding is not honest, but subtle hostility.

Rose N. Franzblau

Sometimes honesty is *not* the best policy. When our motives are wrong, so is our truth. When we "tell it like it is," we in essence are "telling it like *we* are," and if we are hostile, our honesty will bristle with that hostility.

We need to be on guard for people who knock the wind out of us with their honesty. And if we are the guilty party, we need to learn how to express anger in a direct, constructive manner, rather than disguising it and hurting innocent people with our faulty truths.

I need to be honest with myself before I can be honest with others.

AUGUST 17

The most exhausting thing in life is being insincere.

Anne Morrow Lindbergh

Polly, an Adult Child, always left social gatherings worn out from the efforts expended in winning approval from others. Effervescent, witty, she could charm the socks off anybody and usually did. "Isn't Polly nice. She is so interested in people, so friendly." Nobody realized that as soon as Polly was alone, her smile disappeared and self-doubt tugged at her, pulling her into despair. She was sure that someone had seen beneath her facade and had rejected her. She had failed. She is a failure. She is worthless. Depression wraps its cloying arms around Polly and it takes her days to pull out of it.

This kind of insincerity is not malicious or calculating. It stems from our desperate need for approval, and it is terribly exhausting. When we can take self-approval with us, it will not be necessary to put on a performance to make people like us.

Today I will attempt to be sincere in my encounters with others. I will not put on an act to make them like me. I will be myself.

AUGUST 18

A man can stand a lot as long as he can stand himself.

Axel Munthe

Many of us turn the anger at what happened to us as children inward, and it becomes self-hate. Every mistake we make becomes magnified by our sense of guilt. Without help, we live our lives in despair. With help, we can release the outrage that hides within and use its energy to help us heal.

Another kind of self-hate is from causing pain to others. Our conscience will eat at us until we have made amends. Sometimes it is too late to make amends, and all that is left for us is to express our grief for what we have done and then let go of guilt.

I am tending to the unfinished business that robs me of self-respect.

AUGUST 19

If I were given a change of life, I'd like to see how it would be to live as a mere six-footer.

Wilt Chamberlain

In childhood many of us dreamed of being somebody else, *anybody* else except who we are. As time went on and we lost touch with our feelings, we also lost who we were. We hung in limbo, not being who we were intended to be and unable to be anyone else.

We long to be like those we refer to as "normal" people, the ones who had it good as kids, and whose lives we imagined to be perfect, with no doubts or fears, perpetually happy.

As we heal we discover that the people we have idealized are not perfect nor problem-free. We stop dividing people into camps and accept that we are all members of the human race, and that life is not always just.

Today I will not compare myself with anyone else.

AUGUST 20

It's time we have that little talk about the birds and the bees . . .

Parents the world over

"Mom, where did I come from?"

"Well dear, it's this way . . . um . . . when a man and a woman . . . er . . . this little seed . . . I mean egg . . . Johnny, I found you under a rock!"

"But, Mom, Billy comes from St. Louis. Where did I come from?"

(Sigh of relief.)

In the healthiest of homes discussing s-e-x with children is often difficult, but in dysfunctional homes where the sexuality of the parents is often in shambles, children not only don't have healthy role models to learn from, they are often sexually abused.

Many co-dependents have sexual issues that need to be addressed. And with children of our own, we have the additional task of helping them to develop into healthy, loving sexual beings. It's a tall order, but if we believe in ourselves and the process of recovery, we can accomplish miracles.

With the help of my Higher Power I can repair my broken sexuality.

AUGUST 21

I don't like a man to be too efficient. He's likely to be not human enough.

Felix Frankfurter

"Being human" is basically the ability to be flexible. And flexibility depends on how willing we are to bend — not our morals or principles — but our responses to life and people.

When we can bend in given situations, we can also bend back into shape. There is no need to remain rigid for fear of breaking. Recovery gives us the balance needed to bend and to stretch beyond ourselves to embrace the human needs of others.

When I feel inflexible, I will visualize a willow swaying in the wind and will try to let myself become like the willow.

AUGUST 22

I accept the universe.

Margaret Fuller

There is a vast difference between tolerating something or accepting it. When we tolerate something, we keep it at arm's distance. When we accept it, we embrace it.

Let's say we have a friend who phones often and chats for long periods of time. She doesn't ask if we are busy and would it be better to call back later. She just starts yakking and we clench our teeth and listen. But we are not listening, we are waiting for her to wear down and hang up. We tolerate her because we don't want to hurt her feelings. If we were to really accept our friend's tendency to be windy, we would either inform her that we are busy and can't chat, or would pour ourselves a second or third cup of coffee, put our feet up and shoot the breeze with her.

I am learning to be more accepting of my shortcomings and the shortcomings of others.

AUGUST 23

Unless I accept my virtues, I most certainly will be overwhelmed by my faults.

Robert G. Coleman

Before recovery, we focus exclusively on our so-called shortcomings. We have such overdeveloped consciences that even minor flaws can keep the taunts from the past echoing round our heads. "Shame, shame on you!" they shout at us and we accept it as truth.

Recovery allows us to claim our many virtues and to weed out those faults that are harmful to our well-being. The other little quirks — the ones that make us interesting and unique — we may decide to keep. These are the inconsistencies that make us identifiable as healthy human beings in imperfect working order.

I will accept my good qualities and forgive myself for having flaws.

AUGUST 24

In the face of uncertainty there is nothing wrong with hope.

O. Carl Simonton

The odds may be against us. Others may tell us something is improbable, maybe even impossible. We may have no idea of what to expect an outcome to be. But these are not good reasons to give up hope.

Hope can, and does, perform miracles — everyday. Doctors have seen terminal patients turn the course of their illness around 180° and be cured. They can't explain it. They can only marvel at it.

Recent studies have pointed to the fact that when we are in a hopeful frame of mind, certain chemicals within our bodies are released. These substances may be our bodies' natural healers which become available through a positive attitude but become inhibited by hopeless negative feelings.

Hope is free. It doesn't hurt and we have nothing to lose by trying it.

I will apply a little hope to my problems and see what happens.

AUGUST 25

The ever importunate murmur, "Dramatize it, dramatize it!"

Henry James

Some call them their "war stories" as they recount childhood experiences in vivid detail, nonchalantly throwing around images of abuse or neglect that shock the sensibilities of listeners. Why do the tellers of these stories seem so callous and removed from what they are saying?

Those who are unaware of the role that denial plays in dysfunctional families cannot understand that the reality of what happened to Adult Children does not emotionally hit home until we break through denial. The underlying cause for this behavior is that we are still caught in the disease process.

In recovery when we share our stories, we experience grief for our losses of childhood. This heartfelt sharing ultimately allows us to close the book on our unhappy past.

When I care enough for myself to cry for myself, I am on my way.

AUGUST 26

They love the best who love with compassion.

Ellen Anne Hill

The old expression, "She's a tarnished angel," had to be coined by someone sensitive enough to look beneath the exterior and see the beautiful soul of another.

We are all tarnished, some more so than others, and as such need someone to look beneath our dulled surface to see our potential — the person we would like to be. Many of us have only known love that is conditional, love that has been doled out according to a rigid set of rules. This kind of love does not nurture, it checks for flaws and when flaws are found, it turns its back. It turns its back when we need love the most.

Compassionate love runs gentle hands over our surface, wiping away the stains so that we can see for ourselves the beauty that lies within us. And compassionate love does not insist that we be flawless, only that we be open to goodness.

I will be compassionate toward myself and others.

AUGUST 27

Incomplete terminations interfere with new beginnings.

Jacob Moreno

A newcomer upon attending her first Co-dependents Anonymous (CoDA) meeting asked a woman who seemed to have her act together, "I don't want to go through all that pain stuff. Tell me how you got so happy and I'll do it your way." The happy lady wanted to reply, "Well, I mixed a banana with a raw egg, rubbed it on my head, stood on one foot for three hours and was cured." But being kind she explained that she is healing, just the way the others are, by feeling her feelings.

We do not want to experience any more pain, but the discomfort before recovery does not get us anywhere whereas the pain we experience in the healing process eventually gets us out of pain.

I can lead the way for others by my example. If they choose to remain in denial, my only responsibility is to accept that fact and accept them just the way they are.

AUGUST 28

Life is fragile. Handle with prayer.

In a literal sense, prayer is self-talk that we believe to be connected by Power lines to a Source beyond ourselves. Our prayers can be born of despair or gratitude. They can be a quiet conversation as though a friend is hearing us out, then letting us reach our own conclusions. Or they can be requests for answers to what-should-I-do questions.

A Higher Power is whatever we believe it to be and that is as diverse as there are religions. But there is a common belief that God is the force for love in the universe. With His Power we can feel benevolent toward others, forgive those who have hurt us, understand those who differ from us and reach out to help those in need.

I am coming to believe in a Power greater than myself.

AUGUST 29

I'm not O.K. You're not O.K. But that's O.K.

Elisabeth Kubler-Ross

A patient in psychotherapy asked her doctor how his emotional health was. The doctor, a man who had a spinal defect that caused him to walk bent forward from the waist, answered with a twinkle in his eye, "Oh, I get by." The patient looked at his open honest face, at his terrible deformity, and decided then and there that her goal was to reach the level of self-acceptance that this man had obtained. Far from perfect, just mighty comfortable with who he was.

Being comfortable with who we are is what being human and healthy is about. But most of us play the "when I . . . then I . . . game. *When I* lose 20 pounds, *then I* will like the way I look. When I get my teaching degree, then I will feel important." Our self-acceptance is conditional and not very comforting.

I'm okay today!

AUGUST 30

Some folks think they are busy when they are only confused.

Workaholism is admired by society at large. "Such a dedicated soul," they say. And we may well be. But excess work can serve to fill our need to be super-responsible, our need to control and our bottomless need for approval. With this as our motivation, we dig our hole deeper as we struggle to fill our internal void.

Recovery doesn't take away our desire to use our talents, or to be a contributing member of society, it only changes the reason why we stay busy. When we have faced our issues, and done the very difficult work required to heal, we won't need to work our way to exhaustion.

Today I will take some time to get in touch with me.

We usually see things not as they are, but as we are.

Projection is the ability to accuse someone else of our guilt. It's part of the "I'm-cold-so-put-your-sweater-on" syndrome that co-dependent mothers are prone to have.

When we make a mistake, we feel that others now know how worthless we are, that they don't like us anymore and that they have phoned everyone to tell them about our mistake. In fact, our blunder has probably been forgotten or perhaps not noticed at all. What we have done is assumed that they rejected us, just as we reject ourselves when we fall short of perfection. And with this assumption we are accusing *others* of being unforgiving and judgmental, when in fact, it is *we* who are guilty.

We used our unhealthy sense of self as the barometer for what others are thinking. As we heal we will do a whole lot less projection onto others, and mercifully, a whole lot less rejection of ourselves.

It is not fair to others to project my feelings onto them.

SEPTEMBER 1

Suspicion is like a pair of sunglasses — it makes all the world look dark.

Comments and *silent responses* overheard at an Adult Children's meeting:

"Deb, let's have lunch tomorrow."

Why would she want to have lunch with me?

"Pam, I tried to phone you today."

No you didn't, I was home almost all day.

"Lonny, you sure are a kick!"

What did he mean by that??

When we suspect the motives of others who have done nothing other than to make a friendly comment, we would do well to suspect that we are the one with the problem. When we recognize it's our insecurity at play here, we can begin to override the negative self-talk with positive talk. At first we may have to force ourselves to reply, "Yes, I'd love to have lunch," or "Thank you," to a compliment. As our self-esteem grows it will become natural and genuine to assume people mean what they say.

I will try not to read negatives into comments by others.

SEPTEMBER 2

An optimist looks at an oyster and expects a pearl; pessimists expect ptomaine poison.

It never hurt anyone to be optimistic. That doesn't mean that we should skip merrily through life like a Pollyanna. The big picture of life is not always pretty.

To be optimistic is to see the turmoil around us and remain hopeful that if we prevail, things will get better. Optimists roll up their sleeves and take action to improve a situation. Pessimists sit down and moan, "Woe is me. There's nothing I can do, it's hopeless." Doom and gloom are guaranteed with this attitude. Optimism opens our eyes to options. We do have choices.

Without being blind to the reality of life, I will try to keep a positive hopeful attitude about my personal future and the future of the world.

SEPTEMBER 3

This above all, I refuse to be a victim. Unless I can do that, I can do nothing.

Margaret Atwood

When we put ourselves in the role of victim, we have no say-so in our own lives. We desperately need approval and seek it by people-pleasing, people-saving and people-controlling. In doing this we put ourselves at the mercy of others. And often those we choose are chock full of problems. As we spin our web to hold onto them, we don't notice that we are the trapped ones and they are free to come and go.

Instead of taking hold of others, we need to take hold of our own lives and untangle ourselves from the attitudes that induce us to become victim again and again. Recovery releases us from the past and gives us the awareness and courage to stop being victims in our present relationships.

I will no longer be victimized by my past. Today I have choices and I choose to recover.

SEPTEMBER 4

Most people are willing to change, not because they see the light but because they feel the heat.

When the heat is on we don't namby-pamby around, we move! Living from crisis to crisis is a way of life for people from dysfunctional homes. As children we became accustomed to crisis, didn't know there was any other way to live. Imagine a family camped in the middle of a railroad track. They feel the vibration of an approaching train long before it arrives, hear the whistle, see the light. But they wait, do nothing, until at the last moment as the danger bears down on them, they panic and leap out of the way. After the train has passed they gather on the tracks again and wait. Dysfunctional families function like this, seemingly unaware that they do not have to get back on the tracks, that there are other options.

I am learning to solve problems before they become crises.

It is important that people know what you stand for. It is equally important that they know what you won't stand for.

Two-year-old children make it very clear what they will stand for. "You're doing it wrong, Mommy puts my other sock on first." "No! I don't want to share my cookies with Sally." No! No! No! is their affirmation that tells the world they are an individual and they want to be treated as such.

Though we're no longer two, it is not too late to assert ourselves. Most of us have said yes to the wishes of others all of our lives. But we are able to say no to ourselves without a second thought. In fact, our self-denial is so ingrained we aren't even aware that we do. And when we have an assertive thought, we scold ourselves.

When we stop our internal put-downs and start standing up for ourselves, we will be saying yes to a happy life.

No! I will not say yes to others if it means compromising my integrity.

SEPTEMBER 6

It doesn't happen all at once . . . You become. It takes a long time.

Margery Williams

The Velveteen Rabbit is a story about a stuffed animal who longs to be real. As the story unfolds the rabbit experiences love and devotion, ridicule, loneliness, uncertainty and loss. All the while, unbeknownst to the little rabbit, he is becoming real. The story ends with him happily hopping among real rabbits. This is what recovery can do for us.

When we come out from under the blanket of denial that covers our real self, we will begin to experience the feelings we have buried. They are painful but they are authentic and they are from our heart. And in time we will know the joy of being real.

When I find my true self, I will know how good it can feel to be alive.

SEPTEMBER 7

A boy has two jobs. One is just being a boy. The other is growing up to be a man.

Imagine! Just being a boy or a girl. Just playing hopscotch without worrying that it's payday and when Daddy comes home, he will be mean and beat up Momma. Or just having a paper route and not having your $2.43 stolen by your mom for booze. Imagine being a child without the weight of the world crushing the life out of you. Most of us *can* imagine what it would feel like to just be a child, and the thought will bring tears to our eyes. Tears we dismiss with the blink of an eye. We know our loss. We're just not ready to feel it.

In recovery we cry for the child that never got to be. And in this act of love, we are able to grow into the man or woman we were intended to be.

I am grateful for the opportunity to make the second half of my life better than the first.

It's never too late.

IT'S NEVER TOO LATE
In dreams he comes to me.
"I am well, if you need me,
I am here."
I wake feeling loved,
more whole than before.
Last night he said,
"Tell us your story."
His hands gentle on mine.
There is peace in his eyes.
My father returns from death,
bearing gifts life denied both of us.

It is never too late for me to let love in and to forgive.

(Poem by Mitzi Chandler)

SEPTEMBER 9

To be ignorant of one's ignorance is the malady of the ignorant.

Amos Bronson Alcott

Ignorance means to lack knowledge or experience, to be unaware of something. Denial is ignorance, and we remain ignorant because we are fearful of looking at our feelings. This is understandable, but to go through life emotionally dull is a terrible waste of a life.

Some say ignorance is bliss and if we opt to remain unaware, we will avoid pain, but we will be grounded in the past. If we decide to overcome our self-imposed limits, we will discover that recovery has wings and we can fly as high as we choose.

I am growing up, up and away from my past.

SEPTEMBER 10

They are good, they are bad,
They are weak, they are strong,
They are wise, they are foolish — so am I.

Sam Walter Foss

So am I. When we heal enough to identify with the human race, we know we are on the road to recovery. For most of our lives we have felt like another species. Observers, we stood back and watched the behavior of others, making value judgments based on our black-and-white thinking. We attributed God-like qualities to some, while others were judged to be bad.

As we join the human race we begin to see the ebb and flow of human responses. We are imperfect, and as such, it is not always possible to live up to the Golden Rule, but there is another gem that we can turn to when we falter. It's called the Serenity Prayer, and it can light our way.

God grant me the serenity to accept the things I cannot change, courage to change the things I can, and wisdom to know the difference.

All of my life I been like a doubled-up fist . . . Poundin', smashin', drivin' . . . now I'm going to loosen these doubled-up hands and touch things easy with them.

Tennessee Williams

Many of us have fronted our pain with a stance of anger. With our chin jutted forward, we go through life ready to pounce at whatever moves. Our internal rage keeps us as vigilant as if we were in a war zone. And we are. We are at war with ourselves and the "bad" guy is winning.

Our stuffing was knocked out when we were young, and our recourse is to knock the stuffing out of anybody who gets in our way. Fair exchange? Not really.

Our bravado will become genuine courage when we confront the *real* enemy — the denial that won't let us grieve for the loss and betrayal we experienced as helpless children. When we can cry for ourselves, our anger will soften, and we will at last be able to unfold our hands . . .

Today I will not be so quick to put up my guard.

SEPTEMBER 12

She was dangerously ill. Now she's dangerously well.

Doreen discovers that she is suffering from the effects of a dangerous disease. She knows that the cure is to acknowledge the disease and apply certain remedies. She reads the instructions and declares herself well. Cured, she races around in delirious circles contaminating others with her tiny vial of information.

We've all met a Doreen, perhaps we were one early in our recovery. Doreen has a working knowledge of the process of healing, but has no understanding of what she is talking about at an emotional level. She is still in denial, still trying to fix others so she can avoid looking within herself.

Recovery is not about information, that's the easy part. It's about transformation, that's the hard part.

Recovery takes place in my heart, not in my head.

SEPTEMBER 13

A single rose for the living is better than a costly wreath at the grave.

Sue Ellen Crumpett passed away. The funeral parlor is bursting with carnations, gladiolus and even roses. Folks have traveled from as far away as Des Moines to pay their respects. Sue Ellen would be pleased to see how much people cared.

For the last seven years Sue Ellen has lived alone. Ever since Henry died. Arthritis kept her homebound a good deal of the time, and being a social kind of person she missed being with her friends.

Her friends meant to drop by, they had it on their "Things to Do" list, but time just got away from them. Then one day the mailman noticed she hadn't taken in yesterday's mail and he got suspicious.

Yes, Sue Ellen will be missed. But she'll never know it.

I will take the time to show others that I care.

SEPTEMBER 14

The fellow who's always leaning on the family tree never seems to get out of the woods.

We can blame the past for our misery until the cows come home, but we won't find the way out of our misery until we stop dwelling in the past. There is no question that we suffered as children and were helpless to find a way out.

Blaming our parents keeps us stuck in bitterness and resentment. These feelings are as deadly to our well-being as being caught in quicksand, the more we struggle, the deeper we sink. We need to reach for a lifeline and help ourselves out of this quagmire.

Taking hold of our own life and letting go of blame is the way out of our struggle. This frees us to begin looking at how our own dysfunction affects our present life and relationships.

When I stop blaming, I can start reclaiming my life.

SEPTEMBER 15

No farmer ever plowed a field by turning it over in his mind.

When the wheels turn in our head, they won't go anywhere without our help. Intentions are just that unless we act on them, and often we don't. Why? A few of the reasons are fear, laziness, we don't think we can succeed, we don't know where to start or we let others talk us out of them.

Some of us have a tendency to be scattered in our interests and find it hard to stick to one thing before scurrying on to the next one. We need to be focused long enough to see something through, and this may take some going against the grain. As we recover our minds aren't so muddled and preoccupied with things from the past. This frees us to concentrate on the here and now, and to use our energies to turn our intentions into deeds.

Today I will follow through on at least one of my intentions.

SEPTEMBER 16

There's no business like "grow business". . .

Growth. Everything about it is appealing . . . . Well, almost everything. No one likes to feel the discomfort that comes with giving up the role that keeps us, if not happy, at least familiar with the script. Growth requires us to change, and to try out for roles we thought beyond our reach. This takes courage and it takes risk.

Those of us in recovery are in "grow business." We may never see our name in flashing lights, but as the lights flash on in our heads, we know that we are making a comeback in the most important role of our lives — the return of our authentic selves.

A bouquet of roses to me for risking and growing!

The cruelest lies are often told in silence.

Robert Louis Stevenson

Many co-dependents disagree that lying is part of their problem. But lying is something we do so well, we're not even aware we're doing it.

When we smile, although we feel miserable and lost, our smile is hiding the truth. When we say yes to a request to do something because we are afraid to say no, it is a two-faced lie. When someone we know is being maligned by nasty gossip and we say nothing, our silence lies. Pretending is itself a lie, sometimes harmless, but nonetheless a lie. We pretend to enjoy what bores us, pretend to feel confident when we're unsure, pretend to like people that we don't, pretend to understand when we haven't — the list goes on and so do the pretenses.

When we honor our authentic selves and uncover the truth of our lives, we will no longer need to hide behind lies for protection.

When I stop lying to myself, I can stop lying to others.

SEPTEMBER 18

No one is useless in this world who lightens the burdens of another.

Charles Dickens

Dickens used his great talent to enlighten the world about inhumanity and injustice. His stories have touched and offered hope to generations of people. Most of us will not reach such vast numbers of people with our caring, but we will reach many in a lifetime and it is no less important.

We can be of service to others in many ways, but one of the ways we often overlook is to *stop* helping them so they can help themselves. When we jump in and do for others what they should or could do for themselves, we deprive them of the opportunity to become self-sufficient. People grow in maturity and wisdom by doing, not by others doing for them.

I am learning the difference between helping and hindering others.

SEPTEMBER 19

Too much agreement kills a chat.

Eldridge Cleaver

Many of us would rather walk backwards to Boston than to disagree with another person. This is understandable. We grew up in homes where a slight difference of opinion could end up in all-out war. So now if Mary says green is her favorite color and Gary says blue is his favorite, and they ask which of the two colors is our favorite, we mumble fearfully, "Both."

As we grow in self-esteem and let the fears of the past fall away, we can participate in the healthy exchange of opinions and ideas among people.

Differences among people offer vitality and excitement. When we work through differences, we feel closer bonds for having shared our real selves.

Today I will take a risk and express an opinion.

SEPTEMBER 20

You'll never really know what I mean and I'll never really know exactly what you mean.

Mike Nichols

Communication of facts can be transmitted accurately from mind to mind, but the sharing of feelings or subjective thoughts is trickier as there are so many variants. What are those variants? In a nutshell, the variants are as various as there are a variety of people. People differ.

As we listen to others recount their stories, express their pain and share their growth, we may not connect to everything they say, but if we listen with an open heart, we will be listening as well as humanly possible.

I will listen to others with an open heart.

SEPTEMBER 21

You can't make a place for yourself in the sun if you keep sitting in the shade of the family tree.

Our family trees cast looming shadows over our lives and until we begin the process of recovery, we aren't able to find our way out of the darkness. There may be moments when light filters through and we feel its warm glow. We get an inkling that there is something beyond the shadows, but we don't know how to get there.

The way out is to let go. Like leaves, we must let go of the branches in order to make room for new life. Healing is a season of our lives. It is a time of falling, of dying to old ways and of rebirth. When we let go of the past, light shines through the bare branches and we are freed from the dark.

When I hold on to the past, I help create the shadow. When I let go, I allow light to filter through.

Do not take life too seriously. You will never get out of it alive.

Elbert Hubbard

Adult Children and co-dependents grew up in an environment that was often grim as death. And sometimes laughter and frivolity was not the fun kind, but the kind that made fun of others. With this as our reality, we grew up taking life very seriously.

Today we can choose to look our reality in the eye and say, "You need an overhaul!" With the tools of recovery we can bang the dents out, replace the transmission, clean out the trunk, and paint it a bright yellow.

When we look for the humor in life, we still won't get out of it alive, but we will get out of it all that we possibly can.

Today I will not take myself so seriously. I will make an effort to lighten up.

Today is a brand new day with no mistakes in it.

Each morning when we open our eyes and let in the dawning, we have an important choice to make before our feet hit the floor: will we get up on the right side or the wrong side? If we choose the wrong side, we'll have to reach under the covers and drag out our bundle of self-defeating attitudes to dump on our brand new day. If we choose the right side, we can start out fresh and make it a day of discovery.

What we do with the first hour of morning sets the tone for the day. It is a time to listen to music, read something inspirational (comic strips count), play with the cat, take a walk or do whatever it is we do that gives us a sense of quiet, a sense of well-being. We have to get up earlier to make this time for ourselves when we have children or have to dash off to our jobs, but it is worth it. With serenity intact, we're ready and able to take on the challenges of a new day.

I am grateful to have a brand new start each morning.

SEPTEMBER 24

I am socially retarded.

Co-dependent

Beth received an invitation to a formal dinner party. Most of the guests are of high standing in the community, and Beth, a co-dependent, has never rubbed elbows with this crowd. She spends days dithering over what to wear, how to act, what to talk about and what fork do you use when and for what purpose?

The natives seem friendly enough, but she is so paralyzed by the fear of committing a faux pas that she can only grimace her way through what could have been a wonderful new experience. She didn't give others the opportunity to discover her quick wit and the genuine warmth of her personality.

Fear holds us back from trying new things and being ourselves in the process. We are not "socially retarded," but often we are inexperienced and let self-doubt color our encounters with folks we deem "better" than we are.

When I feel inadequate around others, I will try to relax and be myself.

SEPTEMBER 25

This could be such a beautiful world.

Rosalind Welcher

If we want to ruin a day before it has a chance to unfold, watch the morning news. And if that isn't depressing enough, watch a few programs. Television provides us with a concentrated dose of what is wrong in our world.

But this is such a wondrous world with wondrous people in it . . . people of wisdom, gentleness, and honesty — caring people of all colors who wish no harm to others.

Although our beautiful planet suffers from the wounds of human greed and misuse, there is still the song of a meadowlark, the unfolding of morning glories, the chatter of squirrels and hope that we can mend the world's wounds before it is too late.

I will make my part of the world a better place.

SEPTEMBER 26

Do what you can with what you have, where you are.

Theodore Roosevelt

We co-dependents are notorious for comparing ourselves with others and usually coming up short. There are moments when we're up there with the gods, but we are soon dashed back to earth. We expend a great deal of energy flying, falling and picking ourselves up. This repetitive effort gets us nowhere but down and up and down again.

As we recover we can break out of this self-defeating cycle and spend our efforts on growth instead of comparisons. We begin to accept our imperfect selves and decide what we want to do about our shortcomings, and what we want to do with our attributes. Then we can make ourselves into the kind of person we've always wanted to be.

I will make the most of who I am.

SEPTEMBER 27

Nothing is so much to be feared as fear.

Henry David Thoreau

Co-dependents do a lot of whistling in the dark. We *have* to. We are riddled with fear and haunted by entities whose visitations keep our real selves crouched and shivering in the corner. And though we put on a brave front, we watch over our shoulders terrified of the shadows that loom from the past.

There is a way out of this dark place. When we allow the light of a Higher Power to enter our hearts, our fear and self-doubt will be overcome by something stronger, and fear will slowly vanish. When this miracle happens, our courage will be genuine, not just a frightened whistle in the dark.

With the help of a Higher Power I am learning to face my fear.

To teach is to learn.

Japanese proverb

It is a paradox that the more we learn, the less we feel we know. Knowledge expands our world, and in one lifetime it is impossible to comprehend that expanse. We stand in awe at the magnitude of the universe and the complexity of life.

We all have the opportunity to be both teacher and student, or we can choose to be a dunce. When we close our eyes to reality, our minds to knowledge, hide behind apathy and make ourselves impervious to change, we neither teach nor learn, we merely take up space. This is a loss and a waste, especially to ourselves.

Time stretches before us as a void waiting to be filled. Only we can determine if it will remain a void or be filled with the challenge of living.

I will open my mind and heart to knowledge and understanding.

SEPTEMBER 29

Argument is the worst sort of conversation.

Jonathan Swift

To iron out differences in a relationship requires that we be considerate of each other's tender spots *especially* in the midst of disagreements. We need to listen intently to what is said by the other and try to grasp the feelings behind the words. And we should attempt to make our points as clearly as we know how without using the "It's all your fault!" tactic.

Being human, we will be drawn into double-dare arguments, shout our way into a corner and wonder how to get out. When this happens, we should back off and declare a truce until we've cooled down.

I am learning to talk, not balk, with my loved ones.

SEPTEMBER 30

Recovery is progressive.

What wonderful news this is! Until the onset of recovery we were still reeling from the effects of a disease we had no control over. Now we have the opportunity to not only get well, but to continue to progress *up* in our recovery. This is nothing short of a miracle!

Most of our lives have been spent trying to block out the terrible pain we felt at our core. Denial — a snake-oil merchant — promised that his potion would take away our pain, but he didn't tell us that its narcotic effect would also take away the essence of who we are.

Recovery returns ourselves to ourselves. How wonderful it feels to move easy in our skin, comfortable with who we are. This newfound ease gets better every day as healing continues. There are no words big enough to express our gratitude for the blessings of recovery.

THANK YOU! THANK YOU! THANK YOU!

OCTOBER 1

A man who dares to waste one hour of time has not discovered the value of life.

Charles Darwin

Time is the corridor in which we journey through life. We don't know what turns it will take, and we don't know when it will end. We only have now. Precious now.

When we are dull with unhappiness, we aren't able to find what life has to offer. Like a scolded child, we dawdle along, scuffing our feet, not seeing the things of value around every corner. We don't *want* to miss out on life; we just don't know how to find it. Blindfolded by denial, we take wrong turns, walk into walls, fall down and stay there dejected.

Recovery is the hand that reaches down to help us up. When we have discovered our own worth, we become like an exuberant child on a treasure hunt, expectant and open to life.

Time is too precious to waste. I will live each day as fully as possible.

OCTOBER 2

Super-cali-fragil-istic-expi-ali-docious

What in the world does that mean? It means anything that we want to make of it, just as we can make our lives anything that we want to.

For the fun of it, let's try a little game. Using the letters in the word above, see how many hidden words we can discover. For starters, there are pearl, tiger, expert and carrot. There are dozens of choices.

Now look at our lives and define the personal choices we have. There are two main ones. We can stay locked in the past or we can break free of it. If we choose the first, we have the choice to be basically sad or basically angry — whichever one keeps the deeper pain at bay. But if we choose the latter, we can find happiness and love.

I have the choice to live fully or merely exist. I choose to live!

OCTOBER 3

When I waste time, I waste me.

Each of us is allotted a given amount of time in which to explore this thing called life, and none of us knows when that time will end. A relentless traveler, time doesn't wait as we dally along, indifferent to what is being wasted.

Growth is a slow process for all of us, but those of us whose maturation was hindered by childhood trauma have to work double-time for a while to catch up with our development. When we waste time, we throw away pieces of ourselves that haven't been explored as yet. And when we don't grow to our potential, we rob our loved ones, our friends, our communities and our world of the best we have to offer.

I have a purpose in life and I need every day available to me to fulfill it.

OCTOBER 4

Prayer is not asking. It is a language of the soul.

Mohandas Gandhi

There is a quiet place in each of us that knows. It knows when we are not in a right relationship with ourselves, others and with a Higher Power. And from this knowing place there is a longing to repair the brokenness to find spirituality and love.

The language of the soul is muffled beneath the discord of our defenses. Denial allows us to avoid the pain of looking into ourselves, but neither defenses nor denial can quiet the longing and the knowing that stirs deep within us.

These quiet longings are prayer. We may not acknowledge them as such, but they are of a higher wisdom seeking reunion with the forces of love.

I will listen to the prayers that whisper from my soul.

OCTOBER 5

A liar needs a good memory.

Quintilian

Lies let us off the hook, at least we think they do. But do they? It seems that they leave us hanging. Hanging on to half-truths, self-loathing and hanging on to reality by our fingernails. Who needs them? We do. Why? We lie because we are afraid, we are wounded, and we lie because we often don't know what the truth is.

Denial is the creator of all our lies. When we deny that a problem exists, what is left is lies.

As we begin to heal and discover the truth about ourselves, we will spend less and less time pretending at life and manufacturing reality according to our needs. And we will discover much to our surprise that the truth does make us free.

When I feel a need to lie, I will try to understand why and replace it with the truth.

OCTOBER 6

We are looking in the wrong places for happiness.

Robert J. McCracken

Many of us seek happiness outside ourselves. We look for it in a fifth of booze, a half-gallon of ice cream, a plastic bag of drugs, a couple hundred at the racetrack, one-night stands — the list goes on, but happiness doesn't. It is short-lived and we feel short-changed.

"Dummy," we say, "happiness is not out there, it is in here." And as we delve into what it is that makes us search for happiness in wrong places, one day — maybe sooner, maybe later — a light goes on and we understand. The light comes from that spiritual place within us. And it holds everything we need to be happy.

I cannot reach for happiness with my hands, I must reach for it with my heart.

OCTOBER 7

Nobody ever died of laughter.

Max Beerbohm

Laughter is the breath of fresh air we need to get away from the drama of life — the intermission between acts. Life is too serious to be serious about all of the time. We have to lighten up, to laugh, to enjoy, to play, to dance, to sing in order to survive the ordeal of it.

Recovery is not only to grieve our losses, it is to regain our ability to laugh. We were born with it — watch a baby laugh until it drools. We had that sense of joy once, we can get it back now.

I want that feel-good-all-over feeling that laughter brings.

OCTOBER 8

Hear the meaning within the word.

William Shakespeare

The dictionary states that the adjective *whole* means: healthy; not broken or damaged; intact; containing all the parts; a thing complete in itself. *Wholeness,* then, is to possess these qualities.

Co-dependents enter therapy and recovery programs broken and damaged, our wholeness shattered by a disease we have no control over. As we mend we discover that we have all the parts needed to be whole, but they are in a jumble and need sorting out to see just where they belong. After we reach a level of health, our spirituality begins to shine through and in time we become complete within ourselves.

I will let my wholeness shine for others.

OCTOBER 9

To behave with dignity is nothing less than to allow others to freely be themselves.

Sol Chaneles

In a sense to behave with dignity is to mind our own business. When we look at it this way, being dignified isn't so highbrow after all, it's pretty down home. It means letting others be just the way they are, without our say-so in the matter. That's a tall order for those of us who feel that others need *our* recipe for living.

The first person we should treat with dignity is our inner child. When we respect ourselves enough to be freely ourselves, it will be a cinch to do the same for others.

I am learning to let others choose to be who they are. Their growth is up to them, mine is up to me.

OCTOBER 10

Integrity has no need of rules.

Albert Camus

Integrity comes from a respect for life. It is the desire to contribute to the common good, the ability to be just without the dictates of rules.

When we were small, our integrity was violated over and over until it withered. We replaced this critical part of ourselves with a set of stringent rules to be followed at all cost. These tenets, wrought from fear, stated that we must be perfect, we must not make mistakes, we must not show our feelings, we must not trust anyone and we must not tell our secrets. These are impossible standards to live by. We have little hope of regaining integrity with these child-made rules as a guide.

Recovery, then, is about self-respect. When we regain that, we will have what we need to live a life of integrity.

I am learning that integrity is not a rigid set of rules but a value system based on self-respect.

OCTOBER 11

You are free and that is why you are lost.

Franz Kafka

Some people opt to come to the table of life with a platter of rigid dogmas set before them. They are served up doctrine, well seasoned with shoulds and shouldn'ts, and are provided with all of the answers to life. This is well and good for them, but many of us have found it necessary to search for spiritual nourishment elsewhere.

As we grow, we accept the uncertainty of life. For us, easy answers take away the challenge and joy of spiritual growth. And though we often feel lost, we discover a wellspring of wisdom that is available to all who dare to be free.

I accept that there are no easy answers to life.

OCTOBER 12

The only thing necessary for the triumph of evil is for good men to do nothing.

Edmund Burke

The word *apathy* means lack of emotion, indifference, listlessness. Denial could be described with the same adjectives. Many co-dependents are apathetic, but the problem is not that we aren't caring — quite the contrary. Our need for approval at all cost, and our fear of rejection keeps us buttoned up tight. It's safer to pretend than to be real, it's easier to tune out feelings than to experience them. So we slump on the sidelines of life, letting others take responsibility, not because we want to, but because we believe it is all that we can do . . . given our condition. Our apathy stems from a sense of helplessness.

Recovery kindles a belief in ourselves, in life and in our commitment to it. As we grow in confidence and spirituality we take our light from under the bushel and let it shine, shine, shine for the good of humanity.

I am exchanging apathy for action.

OCTOBER 13

Friendship is a sheltering tree.

Samuel Taylor Coleridge

One of the most precious gifts of recovery is friendships. Before, being with people was uncomfortable, and we exhausted ourselves in our efforts to be liked. It was easier not to have friends. After all, if they *really* knew us they wouldn't like us. We felt lonely and isolated, but that was more tolerable than the risk and commitment of intimacy.

When we learn to trust again, we experience the ease that comes with genuine friendship. There is a give and take that flows in harmony among friends.

For many of us our family of origin may not choose to recover and will stay locked in the furor of dysfunction. When this is the case, our friends become even more — they become family.

I am learning to bask in the warmth of friendships.

OCTOBER 14

Afoot and light-hearted, I take the open road,
Healthy, free, the world before me,
The long brown path before me, leading wherever I choose.

Walt Whitman

Our destination in recovery is the open road — our life stretching before us free of the barriers that have constrained us. We have things to do, places to go, people to meet and dreams to follow. And we can travel as far as we dare.

We have many talents that have lain dormant as we struggled to survive. It's time to become what we said we wanted to be when we grow up. We have been loners, now is the time for joining with others who have similar interests, be it bird-watching, square-dancing or mountain climbing.

I am on a road that leads to happiness, and I am grateful.

OCTOBER 15

Whether you think you can or whether you think you can't — you are right.

Henry Ford

"Oh, I can't do that," says she and her mind closes. "Sure, I can do that," says he and his mind opens. *Can't* restricts, while *can* expands our ability to learn, risk, reason, create, and grow. And it is a matter of choice.

"No, I could never talk with my family about being an Adult Child, it would just kill them!" One can almost hear the door slamming shut on the possibility that breaking out of denial could bring new life for the family.

A positive approach to life first assumes that problems are solvable, and second, it opens our mind to search for creative solutions. An attitude that says Yes! is one that is willing to risk failure but is banking on success.

Today I will take a small risk and try something I don't think I can do.

OCTOBER 16

Life is a series of problems. Do we want to moan about them or solve them?

M. Scott Peck, M.D.

All humans are bombarded with problems, big and small. Fortunately for some, unfortunately for others, problems are not distributed equally among mankind. The wisest thing anyone can do with their lot is to tackle the problems, rather than bemoan their misfortune.

Life roughed us up when we were too young to do anything about it. We brought our feelings of helplessness into adulthood and behave in ways that keep us from effectively working through problems. Yes, we have reason to feel cheated out of our childhood, which gives us all the more reason to rid ourselves of its scourge and make the present and future as happy as we can make it.

I am learning to take responsibility for my own life.

OCTOBER 17

The muck stops here!

Mitzi Chandler

We can't help nor change what happened on the road behind us, but we sure as heck can pull ourselves out of the mire we're in now. With a firm tug we can uproot ourselves a step at a time and forge ahead on the Road to Recovery. Not only will we be blazing new trails for ourselves, we will be providing a way around the muddle for our children and their children.

The journey is too important to our lives to stop when the going gets rough — and it will for a while. But we can lean on others who know the way, and we soon learn that although recovery is difficult, it's a whole lot better than the muck we have been stuck in for most of our lives.

My life is taking a new path and I am grateful.

OCTOBER 18

True friendship comes when silence between two people is comfortable.

Dave Tyson Gentry

There is a knowing between true friends that needs no words. Words might even hinder the flow of communication. When two hearts speak to each other, the message is carried through the eyes, in a touch and by the nestling of emotions.

One of the blessings of recovery is forming genuine friendships. The deep knowing that links us with those whose experiences have paralleled our own provides us with great comfort. Sometimes wih a gesture, we know the meaning of what is being conveyed without further explanation.

It is said that silence is golden and the silence that speaks so eloquently between friends is the purest of gold.

I am grateful for the blessings of friendships.

OCTOBER 19

Since I am human and you are human, to love humans means to love myself as well as you.

M. Scott Peck, M.D.

There is a game children play called Telephone. A statement is whispered in a player's ear, and that player in turn whispers it to the next player on down the line. Needless to say, by the time it is repeated over and over, the original message is quite garbled.

For many of us, the message that we should love ourselves became garbled. This distortion continued until we not only thought it wrong and selfish to love ourselves, we believed that it was downright sinful!

The truth is that it is not possible to love others without first loving ourselves. What is precious in others is also precious in self. We need to clear up the garble, it is the wrong message.

I was created to love myself and to pass it on to others.

OCTOBER 20

Better bend than break.

Scottish proverb

When we can't bend, we're sure to snap — snap at others and snap back into old habits. Rigidity leaves little margin for error and being human is to err. The wisest thing we can do about rigidity is to snap out of it.

To bend is to be able to go with the flow of life, sway to its rhythms and bow gently when storms come our way. To be flexible is to accept graciously what we cannot change and to courageously change the things that we can. And when we let go of rigidity, we will know the difference.

I am learning that life is a dance, not a stance.

OCTOBER 21

Ego boundaries must be hardened before they can be softened . . . One must find one's self before one can lose it.

M. Scott Peck, M.D.

Not only do co-dependents have no discernible boundaries, their sense of self is so flimsy that another could walk right through them and not even notice — which, by the way, is what happens all the time. What we need here is some sort of barrier until the untenable ego is strengthened.

When our self-esteem has healed enough for us to venture out, and to allow others in without losing ourselves, we discover that we have options: We can close our boundaries when we deem it necessary for protection, or we can open ourselves fully to the joy of intimacy.

If others enter my boundaries and step on my toes, I have a right to invite them to leave — pronto.

OCTOBER 22

Follow your dreams.

On the journey of recovery we have mountains to scale and rivers to cross on our way to finding ourselves. When we surmount the difficulties, we will discover many rainbows and fulfill dreams we never thought possible.

Taking the first steps of our journey is a leap of faith. We have no inkling of where we are going or how to get there, we only know that others who have found their way tell us that it is a sacred road that leads to a bright new world.

I have faith that darkness will end in light.

OCTOBER 23

Admitting error cleans the score
And proves you wiser than before.

Arthur Guiterman

Many of us wonder why our lives are not working well, why relationships fail, why our children are so troubled. We lament that nobody appreciates what we do for them. We are proud of our high standards, our generosity and we certainly have tried to raise our children with discipline. If others would only adapt to our value system, life would be wonderful.

We learned our value system in another time and place when it was the best we could do to survive. We don't need it anymore, it plays havoc in the here and now and is certainly not worth the price we pay. We need to let go of grandiosity and control, and allow ourselves the privilege of being a mere mortal.

When I admit that I am wrong, I have the chance to get it right.

OCTOBER 24

We are healed of a suffering only by experiencing it to the full.

Marcel Proust

Healing pain is like the pain of giving birth to new life. What is being born pushes through an internal passage, causing intense waves of distress. In time this pain makes way for new life.

When we try to abort grief, we only succeed in internalizing it, causing a numbing that arises from unrelenting depression.

To suffer fully is to be born to new life. While we grieve, we need to surround ourselves with others who understand and who care. It is time to be gentle with ourselves. In time the pain will lessen, and we will begin to feel new life stirring inside, and we know that our Higher Power has performed one of his finest miracles — the healing of a broken heart.

The more I heal, the more I will feel . . . sadness and joy.

OCTOBER 25

There is always free cheese in a mousetrap.

American proverb

Whether it be two hands in the cookie jar, *another* pair of jeans on the over-charged card or chewing on tidbits of juicy gossip, our high will be low-down in no time flat. When we use and misuse people or things to relieve internal conflicts, we are doomed to instant retribution.

Our dilemma is an inside job and as such needs fixing from the inside out, rather than the outside in as we have tried to do umpteen thousand times. When we understand what gnaws at us and why, we can grow beyond the need for quick fixes and experience the rewards that come from patience, discipline and the ability to express and fulfill our needs in healthy ways.

I am no longer willing to settle for quick fixes. I am opting for slow steady growth and the rich rewards that come with it.

OCTOBER 26

If you want to be found, stand where the seeker seeks.

Sidney Lanier

Children love to play hide 'n' seek, but those of us from dysfunctional homes stop seeking early on and spend our childhood and then adulthood hiding — from ourselves as well as others.

We are ingenious at finding places to hide. We take refuge in addictions, in making ourselves indispensable at work, in chronic fatigue and frequent illness, beneath our do-good halo and by our proclamation that we are hopeless. We even discover hiding places in support groups and therapy by going through the motions while denying the emotions.

Some co-dependents are able to bear the loneliness of hiding for all of their lives, while others decide that it is worth the risk to venture out into the open where we can be found. It is a choice between existence . . . or life.

I choose life.

OCTOBER 27

Forgive all who have offended you, not for them, but for yourself.

Harriet Uts Nelson

How, we ask, can we forgive what is unforgivable? The litany of abuse and neglect suffered by codependents is abominable. Why should we forgive those who all but destroyed us?

Forgiveness is the breaking of the chain that binds us to the past. It is our declaration that we are no longer helpless victims, but free souls who want to love and live. When we forgive, we let out the odious breath of hate and bitterness and take in the fresh air of serenity.

When I learn to love and respect myself, I will be able to forgive those who hurt me.

OCTOBER 28

Pity me that the heart is slow to learn
What the swift mind beholds at every turn.

Edna St. Vincent Millay

Our brains are high-tech computers able to process information quickly and store it for future use. That's the easy part. When the input is of an emotional nature, it is relayed to the heart whose job it is to mull it over. That's the hard part and takes longer. "Don't rush me," our hearts protest. "I'm working on it."

If our minds are open to change, we've got a foot in the door. Then it's just a matter of time until our hearts are swayed and give in with a sigh.

I will be patient with the time lag between knowing and doing.

OCTOBER 29

Someday my prince will come.

Maidens the world over

Little girls are taught the fine art of surrender and dream of the day when they will be swept away by a prince on a white horse. And little boys are instructed in the techniques of capture, then fitted into suits of armor to go forth.

Paperbacks sizzle with co-dependent stories in which a stunning heroine saves the soul of a misunderstood macho man. We are bombarded with sick relationships held up as examples of true love.

Genuine love has absolutely nothing to do with surrender versus capture, neurotic dependency, violence, jealousy or possession of another. But if caring love is not displayed in our families and seldom depicted in popular films, literature or song, how do we know what it is? When we learn to love ourselves, we will not accept nor seek love that is not based on mutual respect and integrity.

I will stop looking for love in all the wrong places.

OCTOBER 30

Great deeds are usually wrought at great risks.
Herodotus

Picture this scene: A co-dependent is waiting at a counter to purchase a sweater. Someone else comes up to the counter and the salesperson waits on her first. The co-dependent musters her courage, clears her throat and says, "Excuse me, I was here first." This simple act is in truth, a great deed — a co-dependent spoke up for herself! This is a major breakthrough for those of us who have spent our lives apologizing for taking up room on this planet.

Each risk we take builds on itself and leads us closer to wholeness. Not only are we enriching our own lives, we perhaps are leading the way for others who would dare to grow.

When I risk, I grow.

OCTOBER 31

People need loving the most when they deserve it the least.

John Harrigan

When we fail at something, big or small, we take the opportunity to knock ourselves around for it, and we manage a few additional licks about past and future failures.

In recovery we begin to treat ourselves kindly by allowing ourselves room to be fallible humans. And when the inevitable happens and we make bad decisions or make spectacles of ourselves, we learn to seek nurturing from friends, knowing that they will understand, and will love us when we don't feel deserving.

When I feel unlovable, I will reach out to others for comfort and guidance.

NOVEMBER 1

. . . Any man's death diminishes me; because I am involved in mankind; and therefore never send to know for whom the bell tolls; it tolls for thee.

John Donne

"I'm a grateful Adult Child." That comment baffles those who have not begun recovery, or those in the pain of healing. We wonder how anyone could be grateful for suffering. "Grateful for what?" we chide.

Out of our suffering has come a deepened sense of compassion for the human condition. We know in our hearts about loneliness, abandonment, loss and neglect. Out of our healing has come a heightened sense of joy, and we know in our souls about miracles. Our gratitude is that we have been given the privilege to go inside the heart of life, rather than merely skimming across its lonely surface.

I am grateful for my own healing and consider it a blessing and privilege to be able to comfort others in their suffering.

NOVEMBER 2

Don't cage me in.

All living things need freedom to be what they are. When an animal is caged, its behavior must shrink in order to survive its confinement. A panther will pace in endless repetition in its need to roam, and an ape will turn its back to onlookers as if seeking refuge from human intrusion. Many animals cannot reproduce and others are not able to live in captivity.

Humans need freedom to express our full range of feelings and to expand our minds. When for whatever reason these activities are stifled, we are diminished.

Freedom from the past will be mine in proportion to how much I am willing to work for it.

NOVEMBER 3

Be not afraid of life. Believe that life is worth living and your belief will help create the fact.

William James

Fear begets fear begets fear, and before long there is only fear, and it permeates our very being. This fear was born in childhood. We are afraid that the worst will happen, and our fear is valid, based on past experience.

For instance, if we are in love with someone and fear being abandoned by them, we may hold on so tightly that we choke the relationship to death, and the object of our love will end up wanting out of our clutches.

In recovery we learn to conquer our fear. As we heal, we discover that if we stand up to life and expect the best from it, we will get it.

I will no longer cower beneath the shadow of fear.

NOVEMBER 4

Compared to your situation, mine's not so bad.

Co-dependent

Co-dependents are champions of the understatement, and are experts at making molehills out of mountains.

At a meeting a woman told of how when she was a teenager, she carried a picture of a somber-faced Korean boy in her wallet. American soldiers found this child huddled beside the maggot-eaten corpses of his family. This woman's childhood was horrendous, but she coped by looking at the face of this unfortunate child and telling herself that compared to him, she didn't have it so bad.

In recovery we learn to stop coping with, and start groping for, the reality of what happened to us and how we feel about it. And we learn not to compare our situations with others, that the pain of loss is the same for each of us.

I am learning to be empathetic toward myself.

NOVEMBER 5

Life can only be understood backwards; but it must be lived forwards.

Soren Kierkegaard

There are those who don't feel that it is necessary to examine the past. "What's done is done." "Forget it." "They're dead now, what's the use." So they bury the hatchet. This solution may work for some, but for others, to bury the hatchet means burying part of themselves along with it.

In uncovering the past we are freeing ourselves from it, letting go of anger, hate, fear and sadness.

When we have grieved our losses and experienced our anger, we can then let the loving core within us have expression.

When I look into the past, I am looking for myself. And when I find myself, I will understand. Then I can forgive.

NOVEMBER 6

Recovery is . . . being able to hang onto my own identity and have relationships, too.

Denise McAlister Cook

For the sake of approval co-dependents will walk into a room of people and give pieces of themselves away bit by bit until there is nothing left. When we enter a relationship, we usually do it in one fell swoop! Without integrity to ground us, we bow in deference to the opinions, wishes, feelings and whims of others.

As our self-esteem grows and we find out who we are, how we feel and what we want, we will stop giving ourselves away to others. With integrity intact, we learn to *give of* ourselves to others in healthy ways, and to protect ourselves from the emotional invasion that characterizes co-dependent relationships.

I am learning to stand up and be counted.

NOVEMBER 7

This above all: To thine own self be true.

William Shakespeare

Who am I? The real answer to this question eludes co-dependent people, but we might answer, "I am anything that others want me to be." We have spent our lives apologizing for being who we are, buying approval from others at any cost and sometimes even selling our souls in our hunger for love.

Recovery is discovering who we are, then being true to ourselves. No longer do we need to bow and scrape to others, laugh at jokes we don't think are funny, smile when we are sad, agree with the opinions of others, apologize or accept blame for things that are not our fault.

Who am I? I am a worthy human being and a child of God. I accept the truth of others and I want to be accepted for my own truth.

I will no longer allow others to rob me of my integrity.

NOVEMBER 8

Fate chooses our relatives. We choose our friends.

Jacques Bossuet

. . . And they lived happily ever after.

When we were children, we longed to be part of that fairy tale. We fantasized that our families would be transformed with a touch from our magic wand, only to have our dreams abruptly end when the ugly dragon raised its head again.

As we discover the blessings of recovery, we want to share it with our families, want them to join us in the new lives we have found. But the reality is that we may be the only one in our family of origin who has the courage to come out of the cave of denial. And this is where our story begins.

In recovery groups we find a new family. One in which we face the dragon together. With love and understanding we help to write each other's story so that we live . . . healthily ever after.

I am grateful for my new family.

NOVEMBER 9

Learning to trust is one of life's most difficult tasks.

Isaac Watts

In our childhood we were repeatedly hurt and let down by the adults in our life, and not knowing what else to do, we packed our bag of pain and emotionally left town. Isolated from even ourselves, we lost our ability to discern who is trustworthy and who is not.

Vulnerable and dependent, we are easily hoodwinked into blindly trusting people who are not trustworthy.

As we unpack our bag of emotions and sort through them, we become more selective about who we trust and more willing to trust those who have earned that right. We learn to rely on our intuition about people.

I am learning to trust those who earn the right to be trusted.

NOVEMBER 10

Think like a man of action, act like a man of thought.

Henri Bergson

Many co-dependents get involved in relationships that would scare off Macho Monster. We are oblivious to red flags and don't heed warning signs. "Man, this is living!" we proclaim.

In recovery we discover that we no longer need the thrill of indiscriminate excitement, and begin to think about the consequences of our choices.

To live fully is to be challenged of body, mind and spirit. We can seek pleasure in sport that requires daring and skill like white-water kayaking or mountain climbing. Our minds might perk up with the mental challenge of a game of chess, and our spirits might welcome a walk along the beach in quiet contemplation. But the most exciting and lasting challenge — one in which we should give our all — is to be in a right relationship with ourselves, our loved ones and our God.

I am learning to stay out of harm's way. And I am finding excitement in activities that provide a warm afterglow.

Monkey see. Monkey do.

When those playful animals follow the example of their elders, they are learning how to live a harmonious tree-top life.

But when we small humans look up to our elders for guidance we can be led down many destructive paths. Dear old Dad or Mom may be riddled with internal conflicts. But we don't know this, so we mimic their dysfunctions.

What we do in recovery is to mimic the behavior of those who have found a healthier way to live. By their example and instruction we learn what we are doing wrong and how to correct it.

I am learning how to live a healthy and happy life.

NOVEMBER 12

The events of childhood do not pass, but repeat themselves like seasons of the year.

Eleanor Farjeon

Like parrots mimicking the voices and sounds around them, most Adult Children repeat the behaviors of childhood in an attempt to "get it right." We choose partners and repeat the patterns of co-dependency we saw acted out in our family of origin. We bring our role as hero, mascot, scapegoat or lost child to relationships and wonder why they always go wrong when we're trying so hard to make them go right.

In recovery we break these patterns by letting go. Letting go of the past by embracing it — grieving its losses, seeing its sickness, accepting its rage, knowing its fears and feeling the depth of our need and love for parents who were not there for us. When we let go, we are at last free to forgive.

Today I am letting go. Tomorrow I will be free.

NOVEMBER 13

Faith is the bird that sings when the dawn is still dark.

Rabindranath Tagore

In the wee hours of recovery, when it is dark — perhaps darker than we've ever seen — we need to have faith that dawn will come.

Until we begin to heal, we are like sparrows huddled in a thicket hiding from life. We closed our eyes to the dark and pretended that it didn't exist.

In recovery when we open our eyes to life, we discover a deep pain within. With faith we can endure the tears of loss, knowing that the morning will come when we welcome the sun with a song in our hearts.

I ask my Higher Power to grant me faith and courage to see me through the dark hours of recovery.

Don't know where I'm going, but I'm on my way.

When we begin our journey we don't know what will be, we only know that it has got to be better than what is. This instinctive knowing is the fuel that keeps us going. And sometimes the going is difficult.

Early in recovery we discover three things that we lost in our youth: the ability to feel our feelings, to trust people, and to talk about what happened. To reclaim these losses is to find the key which will unlock the door to a whole new world.

When we begin to share our stories with others who understand and begin to experience the intense emotions that recovery evokes, we are reclaiming our right to feel, to trust and to talk.

I am grateful to be on a journey that will lead to the unfolding of my heart.

NOVEMBER 15

Blame yourself if you have no branches or leaves. Don't accuse the sun of partiality.

Chinese proverb

Our beginnings were impoverished. This is so and there is nothing we can do to change it. We can only change the way we let it influence our lives today. If we hold on to blame, we will remain in the shadows of the past. But if we choose to grow, we can begin to bend in ways that allow us to reach the light.

To acknowledge that our families were dysfunctional and to grieve our losses is not placing blame on anyone. We are not being disloyal, we are being honest and striving to be healthy.

In the here and now we have a choice.

I choose to accept responsibility for my life.

A person remains immature, whatever his age, as long as he thinks of himself as an exception to the human race.

Harry Overstreet

The basic ingredients in cake batter are flour, eggs, oil and sugar. Cakes are pretty much alike until we start adding the spices, nuts, fruits and flavoring that turn them into chocolate or cherry or lemon cakes. But the very essence of them is the same no matter what icing we spread on top.

People are like that, too. At base we are alike. We enter the world in the same way; our internal plumbing, electrical, and pumping systems are exactly alike, but we differ in appearance, intelligence and in the way we respond to what happens to us. We are part of the human race, unique as individuals, but very much alike as a species.

In the important things of life I am no different than other people.

NOVEMBER 17

I will not permit any man to narrow and degrade my soul by making me hate him.

Booker T. Washington

When filled with bitterness, we leave little room for the sweetness of life. Our hate spills out onto all aspects of our lives affecting how we respond and relate to the world at large.

The hate that we harbor keeps our souls constricted, narrowing and corroding our own lives and the lives of those we love.

Many of us were victims of terrible abuse and neglect as children so our anger at what happened to us is justified. When we let go of our rage, we can forgive and be freed to enlarge and enrich our lives in a way we never dreamed possible.

When I hold on to hate, I am hurting myself and those I love more than anyone else. With understanding and the help of my Higher Power, I can let go of bitterness.

NOVEMBER 18

Happiness is the sense that one matters.

Samuel Shoemaker

To believe that we do not matter is to feel isolated and worthless. We harbor the thought that it is of no importance if we exist or not. Carried further, this feeling makes us believe that it would be better if we *didn't* exist. Many people have taken their lives when they could not find their way out of this painful frame of mind.

This feeling of worthlessness is one of the symptoms of depression. Fortunately, many lives are now being brought back into balance with the aid of medication and professional help.

Many co-dependents suffer depression brought about by suppressing feelings, especially anger. We turn it inward and rage against ourselves. When we have emptied ourselves of the pain, we can affirm that we are deserving of love and happiness.

I was created by God and I have a purpose in life. I am learning to love myself and to understand that I matter to others.

When love and skill work together, expect a masterpiece.

John Ruskin

Recreating the images we have of ourselves is like painting over old portraits. We painted distorted self-images when we were young following the descriptions given to us by others.

Recovery allows us to paint over the canvases of our childhoods. As we work, we begin to see ourselves in a new light. We discover that the ugly messages we received about ourselves are not true. We experience love and compassion for the children that we were. Inspired, we dip our brushes into our hearts and paint into the night.

When we stand back and observe our work, we see that we are painting a masterpiece. With the help of our Higher Power we are bringing to life the soul of the beautiful child within.

I am lovable. I am beautiful. And I am a worthy human being.

When you go on a diet, the first thing you're apt to lose is your sense of humor.

Many of us use food as a catch-all for our feelings. We reach into the refrigerator and swallow anger, swig down depression, gobble up fear and scoop our sense of humor from a carton of Rocky Road. And a rocky road it is the next day when we declare war and prepare to die(t).

Recovery is facing the feelings that eat at us. This is not easy, but the rewards gained are well worth the effort. We discover that caring friends can soothe our emotions far better than food, and learn to reach for the phone instead of fudge when we need comfort. We learn to respect our feelings, understand their causes and how to express them, rather than repress them with food.

When we replace the habit of *indulging* with *divulging* to meet our emotional needs, we are on our way to healthy minds and bodies.

Food is nourishment for my body. Expressing my feelings is nourishment for my mind and heart.

NOVEMBER 21

Dancing is the art of getting your feet out of the way faster than your partner can step on them.

There is a variety act that features what appears to be a man and a woman dancing. Actually it is one performer wearing two dummies who are dressed in gown and tuxedo. They move around the stage clinging to each other in an awkward waltz. Co-dependency is like this. The partners are enmeshed, their real identities buried beneath the make-believe dancers and the waltzes performed are anything but graceful.

Recovery allows us to unbend and identify ourselves. When we have done this, we are free to maneuver out of the way of the intruding steps of dysfunctioning partners. And if our partners continue to try to step on our toes, we have the option to refuse their invitations to join them in the painful dance of co-dependency.

I am learning to take care of myself. I do not have to stand by passively and let others hurt me.

NOVEMBER 22

It was as helpful as throwing a drowning man both ends of a rope.

Arthur "Bugs" Baer

As children we took on roles that helped to keep us afloat in the turbulence at home, but our enabling behavior also allowed the problems to continue. Caught in the currents of co-dependency we did not have the knowledge or skills to pull away.

When we enable others to behave in unhealthy ways, it is like trying to pull a thrashing person from the water — more than likely, we will be pulled under with him. Protecting, lying, making excuses and taking the blame on ourselves only allows the people we are trying to save to sink further. We can give them our love, our understanding and our encouragement, but we cannot take responsibility for them or continue to enable them in their drowning.

Sometimes the best way for me to really be of help to others is to *stop* helping them.

NOVEMBER 23

You sang to me Whiskey's Song
You sang my life off key . . .

Mitzi Chandler

In music a transition is a passage that connects two melodies, and it is often done in another key. For co-dependents recovery is the transition period that allows us to find the right key in which to live our lives. Before we begin the healing process, our emotions are in discord and we don't know how to quiet their harsh sounds.

Recovery gives us the skills we need to find the right key. With practice and patience we learn the sweet song of love and learn the harmony of living in healthy relationships with others. And with our healing we will be able to sing beautiful lullabies to the next generation of children, our notes reverberating clear and true.

I am writing a beautiful new song for my life and for those whom I love.

NOVEMBER 24

. . . Each cycle of the tide is valid; each cycle of the wave is valid, each cycle of a relationship is valid.

Anne Morrow Lindbergh

Healthy relationships are dynamic. We cannot expect them to remain the same as we change.

Working together to keep relationships afloat is likened to two people sitting in a small boat. Their weight must be evenly distributed to keep the boat centered. When one shifts slightly to one side, the other must make a slight adjustment to accommodate the change. The oars must pull in the same direction to move the boat forward. If one person stops rowing and the other continues, the boat will go in circles. And if the water becomes choppy, extra care is needed to keep the vessel from tipping over.

It takes compromise, consideration, communication and respect to keep relationships on course.

The healthier I become, the healthier my choices and the healthier my relationships.

If you can't be thankful for what you receive, be thankful for what you escape.

There is a vast difference between minimizing and being thankful. When we minimize what happened to us, we discount ourselves, denying the validity of our pain. Being thankful is to acknowledge the blessings in our lives and realize that there is no life free of pain and problems.

Our all-or-nothing thinking keeps us caught in denial. We rationalize that by comparison, our problems are not as bad as someone else's.

Being grateful for our blessings is healthy, but to minimize our issues indicates that we have more emotional work to do. Our problems matter. We matter. And when we recognize that fact, we are on our way to recovery.

I am grateful for the positive things in my life and I am learning to acknowledge and grieve the losses.

Joy enters the room. It settles tentatively on the windowsill, waiting to see whether it will be welcome here.

Kim Chernin

Like fragile glass objects, moments of joy were repeatedly shattered in our childhood homes. So precious the feeling, so painful the loss, that we stopped wanting happiness. If we expected nothing and felt nothing, then at least we didn't have to feel the loss. And over the years we lost our ability to feel joy. We buried this treasure deep within our being.

When we begin to trust in life again, our fear dissipates and we are able to release joy from its hiding place and welcome it into our hearts.

I will open my heart to the joyful feelings I have locked away.

NOVEMBER 27

I am more involved in unlearning than learning. I'm having to unlearn all the garbage that people have laid on me.

Leo Buscaglia

If we could start fresh at age 25 or 60 — whatever age we are when we begin recovery — it would be much easier than tackling the house-cleaning tasks that await us. We have to throw out the old beliefs and behaviors that clutter our minds before we can begin anew. This takes time and emotional energy, and no one else can do it for us.

When our house-cleaning is done, we can paint our lives with bright colors and rearrange our feelings and beliefs in ways that are comfortable and healthy. Best of all, we can open the windows to our hearts and let the fresh air of forgiveness and love enter to enrich our lives.

I am in a process of cleaning out the old to make room for the new. With the help of my Higher Power and the support of others, I can accomplish my task.

I cannot give you the formula for success, but I can give you the formula for failure — try to please everybody.

Herbert Bayard Swope

"And our next performer is Vicki. Watch her ride a unicycle with a stack of china cups on her head and juggle ten tennis balls while blindfolded!"

For co-dependents this sort of act is a daily feat as we attempt to please everyone around us. We extend ourselves beyond reason to win the approval of others, often neglecting our own needs and responsibilities in doing so. The end result of our behavior is that we fall off our unicycles, the china cups crash around us and the tennis balls bounce hollow until they come to a stop. Still blindfolded, we pick ourselves up, dip into our bottomless heap of cups and balls and begin again. We pray that this time — if we do everything just right — we will succeed in winning universal approval.

Today I will not negate myself to please someone else.

NOVEMBER 29

Not until we are lost do we begin to understand ourselves.

Henry David Thoreau

When we are in a state of denial, we don't fully realize we are lost. We wander through our days in hopes that the next relationship, the next bout of grandiose feelings or the next spurt of willpower will last, and that we will be freed of self-doubt. But when these periods prove to be temporary, the pain and confusion returns and our hopes are dashed.

The day we give up our futile attempts to run from our feelings and accept that we are lost, is the day we begin to find ourselves. Slowly the dawning of who we are unfolds, and we at last see the truths that denial has kept hidden away.

I will not run from myself any longer.

NOVEMBER 30

What is required is sight and insight — then you might add one more: excite.

Robert Frost

A life well lived is a life that is punctuated with joy. If knowing and understanding are the essentials penned across the pages of life, then joy serves as the exclamation mark! When curiosity has us wide-eyed or happiness splashes carelessly out of our hearts, we have given ourselves over to that magical child that lives in us.

As responsible adults we are expected to write the hours of our day with purpose and composure. But without moments scribbled in joyful abandon, life can be bland and tedious.

In recovery we will rediscover the joyful excitement of the child within and rewrite the script of our lives with a pen dipped in rainbow colors.

Joy and the excitement of being alive will be my reward for working through the pain of my childhood.

DECEMBER 1

Holidays mean: anticipation, preparation, recreation, prostration and recuperation.

"Ho! Ho! Ho!" could very well be changed to "No! No! No!" for Adult Children. Holidays were times of high expectations and painful disappointments when we were young. Our wish now is that December would disappear from the calendar. We feel tremendous pressure to overindulge, overspend and overextend ourselves for weeks on end.

In recovery we can recreate holidays in which we find pleasure in the present and peace of mind from the past. When we have done our grief work, the painful memories won't haunt us with such fervor. We can form new traditions or lovingly embrace the old ones. And with our newfound sense of selves, we can say no to too much spending, indulging and commitment.

I am giving myself the precious gift of recovery this holiday season.

DECEMBER 2

Many convictions are family hand-me-downs.

We bring to adulthood a box of convictions about who we are. These were handed down to us by our families of origin. Much of the convictions we clothe ourselves in do not fit but we wear them anyhow. They hang on us like oversized coats, dragging us down or are garments that are too tight, constricting our emotional movement. Our self-images were formed by unhealthy adults before we had a say-so in the matter. We grow up unaware that we can discard these ill-fitting garments.

To heal is to strip ourselves of the hand-me-down convictions, stand naked in the light of truth, then begin to dress ourselves in new emotional clothing that says, "I am a Being created by a Higher Power, and I am beautiful."

I am a worthy person. I will treat myself with respect and kindness. I will no longer let the old convictions shape my self-image.

DECEMBER 3

People-pleasing differs from bringing pleasure to people.

Shirley is in a quandary. She wants to give a surprise party for friends who are celebrating their 50th anniversary. This will involve a great deal of work for her. The dilemma is this: Before recovery Shirley probably held the world record for people-pleasing. Now that she is healing she does not want to behave in the old ways that left her feeling unappreciated and resentful. Is giving this party a means of buying approval or is this something she really wants to do?

It is normal to have an assortment of motives for the things we do. If Shirley genuinely cares about this couple, her reason for giving the party is probably healthy and she should go with that assumption. The real proof will come when Shirley discovers that she feels good for the party she gave, rather than for what she got back.

When I people-please, I am holding on to expectations. When I bring pleasure to people, I am letting go of expectations.

DECEMBER 4

Worry is as useless as a handle on a snowball.
Mitzi Chandler

When we lug our heavy satchel of worries as we pace the floor, fearing the worst, we waste energy and countless hours in imagined horrors. And in our pacing we may not notice that what we are fretting about hasn't occurred or has melted away. If our concern is legitimate, we might spend our time better by taking action rather than being immobilized by worry.

Coming from dysfunctional homes is cause enough to make us fear the worst. Often the worst happened. We became conditioned to this state of affairs but our task now is to pack away the old worry we carry and free our hands and hearts to act and react productively.

I am learning the difference between useless worry and healthy concern.

J. Paul Getty sent the following to a magazine requesting a short article explaining success: "Some people find oil. Others don't."

Finding oil requires risk, patience, persistence and hard work. Finding ourselves requires the same things. The richness that lies at our core is buried beneath the bedrock of denial. To break through this solid barrier and reach our feelings takes courage.

Not everyone can do this. Some of us never begin the search. Others of us may begin, then abort our efforts when we discover the emotional work involved. But those who are willing and able to stick with the process of recovery can succeed in releasing the flow of life that lies within their being.

I will no longer search "out there" for what lies within myself.

We do not stop playing because we grow old.
We grow old because we stop playing.

Rain, rain go away
Little me wants to play

No matter what our ages or emotional states, playing is essential to our well-being. When we can no longer join in on the spontaneity of play, we have lost a vital part of ourselves. We're like a ball without a bounce.

Recovery helps us to regain our bounce. Repairing our damaged self-esteem is like filling a flattened ball with air and tossing it back into the game.

Today I will let the playful child within have some fun.

DECEMBER 7

Only in quiet waters do things mirror themselves undistorted. Only in the quiet mind is there adequate perception of the world.

Hans Margollus

One of the wonderful rewards of recovery is serenity. Before, our thoughts swirled in confusion or raced in frantic searching. The turbulence in our minds made it difficult for us to quiet the troubled waters. Recovery shows us how.

When we stop denying our feelings, our hearts and our minds begin to flow in the same direction instead of crashing against each other like waves against a rocky shore. In this flowing together we at last find serenity.

I am grateful for the new insights I am gaining. With the help of my Higher Power I will find serenity.

DECEMBER 8

The universe is full of magical things patiently waiting for our wits to grow sharper.

Eden Phillpotts

The same universal truth in the quote above is also true about our individual lives. Recovery is the telescope that brings into focus what was blurry in our minds, discovering what is hidden in the expanse of our hearts.

And what we discover *is* magical: the wonder of being comfortable with ourselves; the thrill of not having to turn inside out to please others or seek approval; the joy of having healthy loving relationships and the delight of being able to play spontaneously.

We open ourselves to the most magical gift of all — our spirituality.

I will open myself to life.

DECEMBER 9

Even a clock that is not going is right twice a day.

Polish proverb

"Am I doing this right?" is probably the question asked most often by co-dependents. Unless we do something perfectly, or the way everyone else is doing it, we feel we have failed. Not only do we berate ourselves for what we are not doing correctly at the moment, we run ourselves down for all of our past imperfections.

As we heal we are able to let go of the black-or-white thinking that keeps us wound up tight. We become more confident in the things we do well, accept that we can't do everything just so and realize that it's perfectly all right to be human.

I am learning to be imperfectly human.

Optimism: A cheerful frame of mind that enables a teakettle to sing although in hot water up to its nose.

Many songs are written about looking on the bright side of life and counting our blessings. These songs are popular because they make life more bearable when we can find what is good in the painful things that happen to us.

This does not mean that we deny the difficulty or pain of our problems, it only means that as we work through them, we stand on tip-toes, raise a hopeful head and whistle.

Today I choose to look at what is positive in my life.

DECEMBER 11

It is not true that life is one damn thing after another — it is one damn thing over and over.

Edna St. Vincent Millay

The best we can ask of life is that as new problems present themselves, we have the ability to solve them and move on. But when our feet are stuck in the mire of the past, we can't move ahead.

We've all heard the saying that the first step is always the hardest. That's true of recovery too — except for one little thing. It's not nearly as hard when we realize that in order to free ourselves, we need simply to step out of the shoes that are stuck in the quagmire and walk away toward healthy living.

I am letting go of the past so that I can get on with my life.

DECEMBER 12

How can I die? I'm booked.

George Burns

Vitality is energy. When this energy is utilized in healthy ways, we can look forward to tomorrow with anticipation and excitement.

Co-dependent people use up a great deal of energy struggling with the unfinished business of the past, leaving us weary and unenthusiastic.

Recovery revitalizes. It sparks our feelings and stimulates us to try new ways of relating to others and solving our problems. With this newfound vigor, we have what we need to wake up each morning raring to go!

I have places to go, things to do and people to meet. I'm on my way!

Anger is just one letter short of danger.

Anger expressed violently is dangerous to others. Anger repressed is dangerous to ourselves. Learning how to express anger appropriately is like taming the wind.

Unfortunately, most of us have seen anger grossly misused in our homes and in society at large. Because of this, anger has received a bad rap, and we are afraid of it.

Used appropriately anger benefits our lives. When there is injustice, anger generates energy and the courage to take appropriate action. When we learn to channel the energy sparked by anger to benefit our lives, we are on our way to healthy living.

I will no longer deny my anger nor will I misuse it to hurt others.

DECEMBER 14

Great thoughts always come from the heart.

Marquis De Vauvenargues

The heart has a wisdom of its own. It is a nobler wisdom than that of the mind. Thoughts and beliefs differ, but the heart of humanity transcends differences and beats as one. It is difficult to know the complexity of another's mind, but easy to know the simplicity of another's heart.

As we recover, we will begin to know who we are. We will overcome loneliness and our sense of rejection and abandonment. We will link into the universal wisdom of the heart. This is the gift of recovery.

I will listen to the thoughts in my heart.

The graduate handed his diploma to his father and said, "I finished law school to please you and Mom. Now I'm going to be a fireman like I've been saying to you since I was six."

Gene Brown

Robert Frost once said, "The brain is a wonderful organ; it starts the moment you get up in the morning and does not stop until you get to the office." This quote sums up what happens to us when we face an eight-hour day working at something that doesn't challenge or excite us.

As we recover, we begin to see other options. For some of us it may be necessary to go back to school to get the additional education we need to become an architect or a teacher. For others it may be giving up a lucrative career to pursue something we've always wanted to do.

When I grow up I want to be a ____.

DECEMBER 16

Old age is like climbing a mountain. You climb from ledge to ledge. The higher you get, the more tired and breathless you become, but your views become more extensive.

Ingmar Bergman

Just as it takes time and effort to climb mountains, it takes time and effort to gain the wisdom that comes from having lived long enough to acquire it.

The arduous task of emotional and spiritual growth is like climbing day after day through fog, our vision impaired by the thick haze. Slowly, imperceptibly, the fog thins and distant peaks appear and beckon to us. And we climb further. Rays of light begin to stream through, urging us on until we are no longer cloaked by fog. Breathless, we stand in awe, gazing out over vistas that stretch as far as we can see.

As I grow old, I will grow in wisdom and serenity if I remain open to life and love.

DECEMBER 17

Life is made up of sobs, sniffles and smiles, with sniffles predominating.

O. Henry

Adult Children became accustomed to the excitement of crises when we were young. We felt alive only when good and bad feelings were heightened. We lived on a roller coaster and our emotions climbed, plunged and careened with each crisis. We didn't know how to feel when life was still, so we stopped feeling until the next crisis.

As we heal we begin to find pleasure in just feeling okay. We discover we don't have to be dancing on a cloud or walking beneath one to feel alive. We come to realize that we can just "be" and find contentment.

I am grateful for the emotional balance I am finding.

DECEMBER 18

You cannot be anything if you want to be everything.

Solomon Schechter

Many people keep a "Things To Do Today" list. They scribble down on a little pad the things they hope to get around to. If at the end of the day they can cross off some of the tasks, they feel they've accomplished something.

But many co-dependents have lists long enough to fill a scroll! There is no way any one person could complete all the tasks on the list, but we try.

When we become enlightened, we will roll up our scrolls and throw them away. We will then prioritize a reasonable number of tasks and at the top of the paper we will write in bold letters: ***Slow Down And Relax!***

I am learning to set limits on how much I can reasonably accomplish in a day, and I am allowing time to take care of myself.

DECEMBER 19

You can't drive straight on a twisting lane.

Russian proverb

Denial is a configuration of roads looping through, over, under and around each other. And all of them lead to the same dead end: isolation and despair. To get off this deceptive road, it is necessary to break through denial and construct a new road with truth.

It takes only one family member to begin straightening the co-dependent behaviors that twist through our relationships. When we have found our way out of denial, we lead the way for others who choose to follow us on the road to recovery.

Each day I am breaking the hold of denial and learning how to grow with the truth.

DECEMBER 20

Bah! Humbug!

Ebenezer Scrooge

Holidays are an especially difficult time for Adult Children. The chaos in our childhood homes intensified during the holiday season. The early excitement and anticipation almost always ended in heartache, broken promises and sometimes broken bones.

When we allow ourselves to grieve fully the losses of the child within, we can create a holiday free of the Ghost of Christmas Past. With childlike wonder we can make the magic come true.

God bless us every one.

Tiny Tim

DECEMBER 21

It is not only the most difficult thing to know one's self, but it's the most inconvenient.

Josh Billings

Henry Ford once said, "Don't find fault, find a remedy." The only permanent remedy for the dilemma in which we find ourselves is to take responsibility for our own happiness and well-being.

Who am I? How do I feel? What am I afraid of? Why am I unhappy? Why do I need to control others? Why am I so dependent on others? Why don't I like myself? Why am I so hard on myself? The only way to find the answers to these important questions is to look within and pull the truths to the surface where they can be understood. We may not always like what we learn. We will experience pain. But we will emerge from the ordeal with self-awareness.

I am learning to be responsible for my own happiness.

DECEMBER 22

Results! Why, man, I have got a lot of results. I know several thousand things that don't work.

Thomas Edison

Learning what *not* to do in a given situation is every bit as important as learning what should be done. Co-dependents have a tendency toward feeling like failures when we make mistakes. When we feel as though we failed, we aren't concentrating on what we learned. So we make the same mistakes over again.

Think of the wisdom we gain when we learn what love *isn't.* This knowledge can change the course of our lives. Time and time again, many of us have pursued what we thought to be love, only to be sorely let down. Until we learn that love does not mean being dependent upon or in control of others, we will continue to repeat the behaviors that keep real love out.

I will start a mental "How Not To" list and add to it each day.

DECEMBER 23

. . . I finally figured out the only reason to be alive is to enjoy it.

Rita Mae Brown

Life has a habit of sneaking up and rattling our cages just when we have settled in and made ourselves comfortable. There is very little we can do about things that happen outside of our control, like someone rear-ending our car or losing a job because the office or plant is forced to close down or the death of someone close to us. When we are healthy of mind and body, we have what we need to deal with the interruptions in our lives.

In spite of its myriad problems, life is full of things to enjoy, big and small. When we accept that this is an imperfect world, full of injustices — some of which we can do nothing about — we are better able to get on with the business of enjoying the little pleasures in our daily lives.

I am learning to enjoy my life in spite of the difficulties.

I am a part of all that I have met.

Alfred, Lord Tennyson

Co-dependents hold on for dear life to the memory of a smile that said, "I like you." A look that said, "I understand." A touch that said, "I feel your pain." One woman recalls that when she was eight, sobbing on the porch steps when her parents were fighting, a neighbor would call and invite her over to make fudge. Another woman remembers that the first time she felt good about herself was when a teacher in the reform school she was in looked at her with love and said, "You're going to make it, girl."

We can never repay those caring people for their compassion. But we can pass it on to other little ones who happen across our paths today.

I thank God for the people who helped me believe in myself when I was a child.

God is home. We are in the far country.

Meister Eckhart

In the womb before we took our first breath, the Hands that created us gently lifted a glistening shape from within our being. "This is your soul. I will take it home." An impression remained where the shape had been, and in it glowed a flicker of light. "This light I leave with you. With it you will find your way to me." And so we come into the world with a deep longing to find our way back home.

As we leave the innocence of childhood many of us lose touch with this holy longing, and instead feel it as a gnawing loneliness. We search for something to fill the emptiness. We run to the end of the far country, and when we can run no more, we see the flicker, hear the words and remember the promise. Born anew, we take our first steps toward the Light.

I am on a journey toward my Higher Power.

DECEMBER 26

How I like to be liked, and what I do to be liked!

Charles Lamb

Co-dependents not only like to be liked, we *need* to be liked, and oh, what we do for approval! And oh, how we dislike ourselves for doing it!

As we recover and gain self-approval, we stop contorting ourselves for the approval of others.

When we like ourselves, it shows. Others are drawn to us without our even trying. We learn that there is nothing we have to do to gain friends, except respect them and let them be who they are.

As I learn to care about myself I will give up my *need* to be liked and replace it with a healthy desire for nurturing friendships.

DECEMBER 27

Life is not a "brief candle." It is a splendid torch that I want to make burn as brightly as possible before handing it on to future generations.

Bernard Shaw

Many co-dependents are intense in nature. Whatever we do, we charge forth with our whole being. Chivalrous knights, dressed in the armor of denial, we gallop through life unable to relinquish the reins until we are thrown abruptly to the ground.

Recovery gives us a new direction for our intensity. Free from the constraints of our armor, we can move freely through life giving each moment, each encounter, the best of ourselves. Using the intensity with which we are blessed, we *can* dream the impossible dream and remain open to the many possibilities of life.

I am grateful that my torch burns brightly.

DECEMBER 28

Some cause happiness wherever they go; others whenever they go.

It is the holiday season and Sara's two widowed aunts are coming for a visit. Sara is eight and remembers she liked one aunt better than the other but can't remember why.

When Aunt Clara and Aunt Jodi arrive, Sara shows them to their room. Clara plops in a chair with a sigh and complains about the long drive. Jodi smiles and asks Sara if she would play the piano for her, that she understands that Sara is getting quite good.

For the next three days Clara takes issue with anything anyone says and scrunches her face when Sara giggles.

Jodi makes a snowman with Sara and hugs her when she giggles.

When it is time for her aunts to leave, Sara wishes that only Aunt Jodi will come back to visit.

I want to be a positive force in the lives of others.

DECEMBER 29

If I had kept my mouth shut, I wouldn't be here.

Sign on a mounted fish

When it comes to advice, wisdom consists of this: knowing when and when not.

There is a big difference between wise counsel and giving advice when someone has asked for your opinion, or when giving it uninvited. When we tell someone what to do about a situation, we rob them of the opportunity to think, to problem solve and to learn. We perpetuate co-dependency. Theirs and ours.

When we have the urge to open our mouths to advise, perhaps it would be wiser to close it quickly and open our ears instead. Nobody's ever been caught with his foot in his ear.

Today I will help others and myself by listening rather than telling them what to do.

DECEMBER 30

Our work brings people face to face with love.

Mother Teresa

Our task as co-dependents is first to search inward for what stands in the way of our ability to love ourselves, then to reach out to others who are still lost and in pain. There are millions of us, and millions of children to come who will enter adulthood ravaged by the effects of living in troubled homes.

Although disguised in grown-up clothes, we recognize other Adult Children in a room of strangers. Something in their demeanor alerts us and we *know* who they are.

We are brothers and sisters, a family of people who understand each other. And in this understanding, we discover love. And we are grateful.

I will reach for help when I need it, and I will reach out to help when I see the need.

Year's end is neither an end nor a beginning but a going on, with all the wisdom that experience can instill in us.

Hal Borland

At midnight on New Year's Eve a silent exchange takes place. On the moment both hands of the Great Clock stand together, the Past bestows its knowledge upon the Future. The continuum comes full circle with but a brief pause to acknowledge an ending and a beginning.

And so it is with our individual lives. We will carry with us into the coming year all we have gathered from the past twelve months and use it to continue our journey. As we wait for the pendulum to swing from the old year into the new, we are granted a moment to reflect. And when the clock strikes twelve, its chimes reverberate our feelings of sadness and joy for what was, and our hopes and dreams for what will be.

With continued recovery, I can look forward to a Happy New Me!

Personal Notes

Personal Notes

Personal Notes

Personal Notes

My Personal Affirmations

My Personal Affirmations

My Personal Affirmations

My Personal Affirmations